WILLIAM CARLOS WILLIAMS' POETIC RESPONSE TO THE 1913 PATERSON SILK STRIKE

WILLIAM CARLOS WILLIAMS' POETIC RESPONSE TO THE 1913 PATERSON SILK STRIKE

Paul R. Cappucci

Mellen Studies in Literature/
Poetic Drama and Poetic Theory
Volume 222

The Edwin Mellen Press
Lewiston•Queenston•Lampeter

Library of Congress Cataloging-in-Publication Data

Cappucci, Paul R.
   William Carlos Williams' poetic response to the 1913 Paterson silk strike / Paul R. Cappucci.
      p. cm. -- (Mellen studies in literature. Poetic drama and poetic theory ; v. 222)
   Includes bibliographical references and index.
   ISBN-0-7734-6912-5
      1. Williams, William Carlos, 1883-1963. Paterson. 2. Williams, William Carlos,
   1883-1963--Political and social views. 3. Strikes and lockouts in literature. 4. Paterson
   (N.J.)--In literature. 5. Silk industry in literature. I. Title. II. Series.

   PS3545.I544 P3327 2002
   811'.52--dc21

                                                                                    2002033657

This is volume 222 in the continuing series
Mellen Studies in Literature/
Poetic Drama and Poetic Theory
Volume 222 ISBN 0-7734-6912-5
MSL/PDPT Series ISBN 0-7734-4159-X

A CIP catalog record for this book is available from the British Library.

The Edwin Mellen Press
Box 450
Lewiston, New York
USA 14092-0450

The Edwin Mellen Press
Box 67
Queenston, Ontario
CANADA L0S 1L0

The Edwin Mellen Press, Ltd.
Lampeter, Ceredigion, Wales
UNITED KINGDOM SA48 8LT

Printed in the United States of America

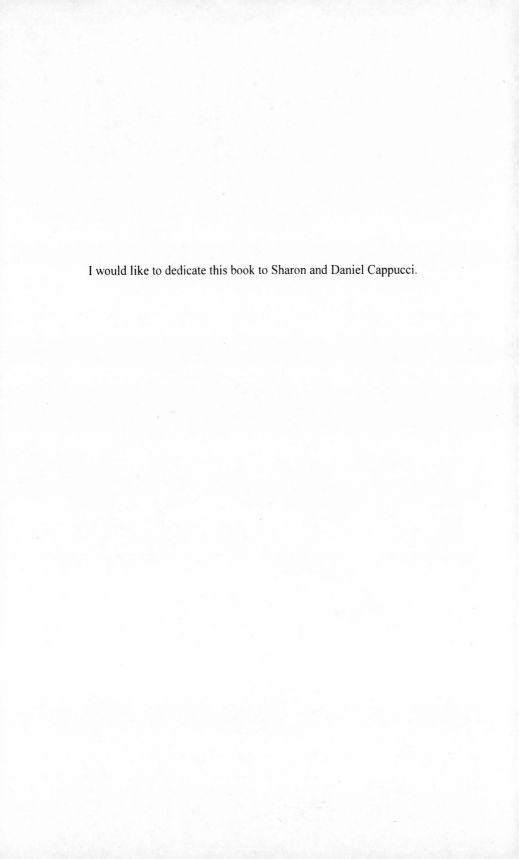

I would like to dedicate this book to Sharon and Daniel Cappucci.

TABLE OF CONTENTS

Commendatory Preface

For many readers William Carlos Williams is the poet of red wheelbarrows, purplish bushes struggling into spring, enduring pink locusts, and Christmas greens. For Paul Cappucci, he is the ambitious poet of *Paterson*. Cappucci's Dr. Paterson is personified so that he can be known and can know himself. Williams grows into that book, that longed-for climax to a life's work, that always-unfinished vision that year by year recedes before him, by finding himself in Northern New Jersey in 1913. In this *annus mirabilis*, Williams became a husband, an expectant father, a householder, an experienced physician, and a privileged observer of the political event of the year: the Paterson silk mill strike. What that strike did for Williams was to anchor his attention to *home ground* and then supply a nearby New York artistic community who found this home significant. For Williams the strike melded radicals, workers, and artists into lifework he could claim: to mirror this modernity, this vilest swill hole in Christendom, through his poems.

After the Paterson silk mill strike William Carlos Williams finally saw how he could also fuse the disparate parts of himself. He could be a particular *kind* of poet, partially modeled by Walt Whitman, who would discard the tired old forms and sounds of traditional British poetry in order to sound his barbaric yawp over the roofs of *his place*: Paterson. He had the image of this encircling flight by the end of the year and published it in "The Wanderer", as Cappucci shows us here.

Whitman seems to me important to Williams in still another way. He centrally validated the poetry of *touch*, of healing touch and thrilling touch. That's the poetry Dr. Williams could write: no ideas but in things. As a physician to the poor, he knew that touch, not knowledge, heals. Thus while living as both poet and physician, the doctor could become the one who transforms the broken or degraded or infected into beauty. Like Whitman he ceases not till death *because* his words can touch and lift up the beautiful things in his world who have been beaten and raped. It is a messianic impulse; thus he is baptized in, or marries as his calling and vocation, or absorbs into himself, the polluted Passaic River, at the end of "The Wanderer."

The Paterson strike of 1913 focused a young bridegroom's attention on stirring facts of life in his locale. Thereafter he saw its moving dramas and the poems which might touch it, the sordid and beautiful people who were its principle players, the sited squalors of its enduring worth. His task thereafter, whether as physician or wordsmith, was to heal by touching. More radically, however, he would also consent to *be touched by* such damaged and beautiful things. He would become them as he expressed them. The allowed this physician to heal himself.

Merrill Maguire Skaggs

Acknowledgements

Grateful acknowledgement is given to New Directions Publishing Corporation for permission to quote from the following copyrighted works of William Carlos Williams.

THE AUTOBIOGRAPHY OF WILLIAM CARLOS WILLIAMS, copyright © 1951 by William Carlos Williams

THE COLLECTED POEMS OF WILLIAM CARLOS WILLIAMS, 1909-1939: VOLUME I, copyright ©1938 by New Directions Publishing Corp., Copyright © 1930, 1931, 1933, 1937, 1938, 1939, 1951, 1952 by William Carlos Williams

THE COLLECTED POEMS OF WILLIAM CARLOS WILLIAMS, 1939-1962: VOLUME II, Copyright ©1944, 1948, 1949, 1950, 1951, 1952, 1953 by William Carlos Williams; copyright ©1954, 1955, 1956, 1957, 1959, 1960, 1961, and 1962 by William Carlos Williams.

THE COLLECTED STORIES OF WILLIAM CARLOS WILLIAMS, copyright ©1938 by William Carlos Williams.

I WANTED TO WRITE A POEM, copyright ©1958 by William Carlos Williams.

Several libraries have been helpful in my research. In particular, I am
grateful to the Rutherford Free Public Library. I am also grateful to Dr. James
Fraser of Fairleigh Dickinson University Library. I also would like to thank the
Yale Collection of American Literature, Beinecke Rare Book and Manuscript
Library. The Rose Memorial Library staff of Drew University and the Sister
Mary Joseph Cunningham Library staff of Georgian Court College also have been
very helpful. I am especially grateful to Mrs. Catherine Stecchini. Her pictures,

memories, and correspondence from Williams provided me with a humanizing view of the poet.

I would like to thank those professors who provided the guidance I needed to develop this book. Dr. Robert Ready provided perceptive commentary and thought provoking questions that enhanced the initial manuscript. Dr. Merrill Skaggs offered constant encouragement and sharp critical insights concerning the project. I feel truly blessed to be associated with her. I would like to thank my colleagues at Georgian Court College who have provided a wonderfully supportive environment. I also would like to give a special thanks to Dr. John Woznicki who showed me the way!

I am particularly grateful to my mother- and father-in-law, Joan and Thomas Dowd, who shared with me their amazing stories about growing-up in Paterson. Not only did they teach me things about the city that you can't find in books, they also taught me profound lessons about life, love, and family. All of my brothers and sisters have been a steady source of encouragement throughout the writing of this book. My parents, Gabriel and Joan Cappucci, also have provided me with a lifetime of love, support, and encouragement. My father's spirit was an inspiring force throughout the early composition of this book; my mother's steady faith and friendship have enabled me to strengthen the current version of it.

Finally, I would like to thank Daniel Thomas Cappucci and Sharon Mary Dowd Cappucci. Daniel has been the joy of my life through the writing of this book—he is instant sunshine when he walks into a room piled with books and papers. Sharon has been there every step of the way. She took the photograph of the Paterson Falls which graces the front cover of this book. She also has been a careful reader, sensitive critic, and Microsoft Word guru. She is the main reason that this book exists. She has revealed to me what is truly possible with "love." I continue to be in awe of her.

ABBREVIATIONS

The references to William Carlos Williams' works are abbreviated as follows:

A—*The Autobiography of William Carlos Williams*

CP1—*The Collected Poems, Vol. 1 1909-1939*. A. Walton Litz and Christopher MacGowan, eds.

CP2—*The Collected Poems, Vol. 2 1939-1962*. Christopher MacGowan, ed.

CS—*The Collected Stories of William Carlos Williams*.

EP/ WCW—*Pound/ Williams: Selected Letters of Ezra Pound and William Carlos Williams*. Hugh Witemeyer, ed.

I—*Imaginations*. Webster Schott, ed.

IAG—*In the American Grain*.

INT—*Interviews with William Carlos Williams*. Linda Welshimer Wagner, ed.

IWWP—*I Wanted to Write a Poem: The Autobiography of the Works of A Poet*. Edith Heal, ed.

P—*Paterson*. Christopher MacGowan, ed.

RI—*A Recognizable Image: William Carlos Williams on Art and Artists*. Bram Dijkstra, ed.

SE—*Selected Essays*.

SL—*Selected Letters*. John Thirlwall, ed.

WCW/ JL—*William Carlos Williams and James Laughlin: Selected Letters*. Hugh Witemeyer, ed.

INTRODUCTION

William Carlos Williams stands as one of the most important contributors to the development of American poetry in the twentieth century. Like Walt Whitman, he was fiercely obsessed with creating a poetry that reflected not only his modern times, but also the language of his diverse nation. He viewed traditional meters and poetic structures as restrictive and believed that a new poetry needed to be grounded in the social and economic reality of his modern world. As he explains in "The Poem as a Field of Action," "what we are trying to do is not only to disengage the elements of a measure but to seek (what we believe is there) a new measure or a new way of measuring that will be commensurate with the social, economic world in which we are living as contrasted with the past" (SE 283). An examination of this social and economic reality can provide us with an understanding of the socio-historical context that informed Williams' poetry production. But, as Williams' words about finding a new measure suggest, this socio-historical approach can also provide us with a clearer understanding of the influences behind the stylistic innovations that Williams achieves in his poetry.

Rather than go off to Europe like his friend Ezra Pound or his enemy T. S. Eliot, Williams purposefully stayed in America to create his verse. His work as a physician in Rutherford, New Jersey enabled him to observe closely the social and economic conditions of the people who lived in the surrounding region. In time his poetry recreated the common details of this locale, whether it was the sound of the broken-English spoken by a Polish patient, the sight of a broken green glass bottle behind a hospital, or the smell of the polluted Passaic River. His use of these details resulted in a poetry representative of his modern American locale.

The value Williams invested in his locale focused his poetic development. He soon believed that "[i]f Americans are to be blessed with important work it will be through intelligent, informed contact with the locality which alone can infuse it with reality" (RI 68). To create poetry out of the materials that constitute industrialized northern New Jersey is easier said than done. Nevertheless, in time Williams saw the poetic potential of the region. It appeared in the old man gathering dog lime, the young housewife moving around her home in a negligee, and even the "Beautiful Thing" getting punched in the nose by the guys from Paterson. These representations of his locality become his own distinct expression of "American" poetry.

In the context of his development as a poet, 1913 was a pivotal year for William Carlos Williams. Not only was it important in regard to the changes in his personal life, but the year also included revolutionary events that influenced Williams's development as a poet. During February the Armory Show exhibition occurred in New York and heralded the modernist movement. At the same time a silk strike of almost 25,000 workers began in Paterson, New Jersey that would last until the end of July. Its initial impact on Williams is evident in "The Wanderer: A Rococo Study," which was published in 1914. These personal, artistic, and social events contributed to Williams' poetic development.

To understand Williams' transformation during 1913, we must first look to the changes occurring in his personal life. On December 12, 1912, Williams married Flossie Herman, and by the summer of 1913 the couple was expecting their first child. During the early portion of the year, the newlyweds rented a room next door to Williams' office, which remained in his parents' house on

Passaic Avenue. By November 1913, the young couple had purchased and moved into a house at 9 Ridge Road in Rutherford. So in 1913 the thirty-year-old Williams was adjusting to life as a husband and homeowner, preparing to take on the role of a father, and balancing his dual occupation as doctor and poet.

Artistically, Williams continued working toward an original poetic style. In March 1913, he reread Walt Whitman's *Leaves of Grass* that he received as a gift from Flossie. At the end of the year, he also published his second book of poetry, *The Tempers*, which included poems written prior to 1913 and some written earlier that year. Williams' encounter with the Armory Show exhibition is another important artistic experience of 1913. In his *Autobiography*, he writes about the exhibition:

> I went to it and gaped along with the rest at a "picture" in which an electric bulb kept going on and off; at Duchamp's sculpture (by "Mott and Co."), a magnificent cast-iron urinal, glistening of its white enamel. [. . .] The "Nude Descending a Staircase" is too hackneyed for me to remember anything clearly about it now. But I do remember how I laughed out loud when first I saw it, happily, with relief. (134)

Flossie did not recall Williams' attendance at the 1913 show and believed that he confused it with another art exhibition held in 1917 (Mariani 106). Paul Mariani, Williams' biographer, finds it "difficult to believe that Williams missed the Armory Show [. . .] since he was frequently in New York then and because even by 1913 he was so intensely interested in what was happening in the world of art" (106). He points out that the show functioned as an artistic "vortex" attracting enormous media coverage. Although uncertainty exists about his actual attendance at the show, it can be assumed that Williams knew about the artistic innovations presented during the exhibition. His awareness of the show's revolutionary spirit, coupled with his own desire to be innovative, no doubt motivated him to take chances in his own verse.

The Significance of A Labor Strike

The Paterson silk strike also began in February. The strike rocked the social and economic structure of Paterson and received widespread media coverage. The strike's initial impact on Williams appears in "The Wanderer: A Rococo Study," which first appeared in *The Egoist* in March 1914. Williams declared this poem to be "the genesis of *Paterson*" (INT 76). Such a direct correlation between the two poems makes a study of the 1913 Paterson silk strike and "The Wanderer" a crucial part of understanding Williams' development as a poet. This poem includes the jarring central section, "Paterson—The Strike," that depicts the crudeness and brutality of silk strikers on a bread-line; it thus shows Williams' willingness to use politically charged images from his locale in his poetry. This section's appearance serves as a marker: it is the point in Williams's development when he realizes that if he wants to create genuine American poetry, he must no longer imitate others, but needs to work with the local subjects available to him.

The 1913 Paterson silk strike not only influenced one section of one poem but also served as a catalyst for Williams as he worked to express his thoughts about America in his poetry. Although poetic imitation did not end at once, poems like "The Wanderer," "Pastoral," and "Portrait of a Woman in Bed" demonstrate Williams' social awareness and use of local American materials. This focus on common material, with its inherent social consciousness, appears consistently throughout Williams' book of poems *Al Que Quiere!* (1917), *Sour Grapes* (1921), and *Spring and All* (1923). In the collection called *The Descent of Winter* (1928), there is still talk "of the strike/and cash" (CP1 299).

During the 1930s Williams' social awareness intensified. He joined the Social Credit Movement and delivered a speech on the topic at a conference in Virginia. His poetry also assumes a much more critical social slant, especially in *An Early Martyr and Other Poems* (1935), with such works as "An Early Martyr," "Proletarian Portrait," and "The Yachts." A short story from this period, "Life

Along the Passaic River," also mentions "the big strike at the textile mills [. . .]" (CS 114). During these years Williams also struggled to compose his epic poem. Explaining his poetic ambitions about using this local place, he wrote to Pound in 1936: "there's that magnum opus I've always wanted to do: the poem PATERSON" (SL 163). Williams worked toward his "magnum opus" for years prior to creating *Paterson*. For example, he wrote "Paterson" (1927), "Paterson: Episode 17" (1936), and "Paterson: The Falls" (1944). Yet Williams did not begin publishing his epic until after the country survived the Depression and World War II.

Despite the passage of time, Williams never forgot the 1913 silk strike. Perhaps the recollection of this event appears most clearly with his use of lines from the "Paterson—The Strike" section of "The Wanderer" in *Paterson* Book II (1948) to describe the working people of the city on their day-off. He also mentions the strike in Book III of *Paterson* (1949). He describes the fall of Catholina Lambert, a Paterson silk manufacturer and owner of a castle overlooking Paterson. Williams juxtaposes Lambert's booming declaration of absolute power over labor with a letter from Robert Carlton Brown that recalls the 1913 strike, John Reed, and the Paterson Strike Pageant. Immediately following this letter, Williams writes about Lambert: "They broke him all right" (P 99). As evident by his use of "The Wanderer" and references to Lambert, Reed, and the Pageant in *Paterson*, the importance of the silk strike stayed with Williams for some time.

The influence of the 1913 Paterson silk strike on Williams has received critical attention. John Thirlwall, who interviewed Williams, claims that Williams "had been impressed by the strike [. . .]" (260). He offers a brief summary of the event and he concludes, "the Paterson silk strike evoked 'The Wanderer' and then *Paterson*" (261). James Breslin argues that when discussing the forces that contributed to the changes in Williams' work, "such matters as the Paterson silk strike of 1913 [. . .] must be taken into account" (18-19). Rod

Townley also sees the silk strike as an influential event in Williams' shift of allegiance from the "elite sect of distanced contemplation and withdrawal" to the "cult of experience" (68). He claims,

> No doubt Williams was helped in this shift of allegiance by having witnessed the Paterson silk strike of 1913 [. . .] and by a new reading of Whitman's *Leaves of Grass*. These too were fires.

These studies mention the strike's importance, but they do not offer an in-depth analysis of what makes this five-month period so important to Williams.

Several other critics focus more specifically upon the strike's influence on Williams. Martin Green's study about the Armory Show and the Paterson Strike Pageant connects Williams' development to this time period. He labels Williams and Dorothy Day as "truer heirs of the spirit of 1913 than those who actually participated in the events of that year [. . .]" (230). He believes that Williams, in particular, epitomizes the reaction "against the 'pure' modernism of Duchamp and Eliot, back toward John Reed and the spirit of 1913" (232-233). Green's insightful study places Williams in the context of his times, especially through his brief interpretation of "The Wanderer," but he does not explore the lasting ramifications of this event on Williams. David Frail's study *The Early Politics and Poetics of William Carlos Williams* offers a more in-depth examination of Williams and the year 1913. Although Frail assumes that Williams had no personal contact with either the New York intellectuals or Paterson strikers during the strike, he does admit that there is a "lack of positive proof against any city activity" (61). He also asserts that Williams was most likely aware of the strike (58). Frail, however, does not interpret "The Wanderer" in the context of the 1913 strike; he contends that Williams probably based the poem on the workers' post-strike hardships (89). Nevertheless, his chapter on 1913 concludes by aligning Williams with the spirit of the times: he describes Williams "captivated by the same sense of possibility as Reed, the pageant, and the Armory Show, and he was no less eager than the fair-haired boys of Bohemia to serve mill workers and bosses alike with poetry as forceful as a citywide strike" (67). Andrew Lawson also discusses the strike's significance in a recent study. He dismisses Frail's contention about "The Wanderer" and the 1913 strike. He argues that Williams's poem "makes use of the spectacle of human suffering, of wasted and alienated labour, to guide it towards a recognition of the profound divisions within the modernity it discovers and mirrors [. . .]" (16).

These critics have discussed Williams and the strike, but more work is needed to gain a clearer understanding about why Williams portrayed it and how it influenced his poetry. Instead of mentioning this event and passing on, this study will take a detailed look at its social, historical, and cultural implications. This study will thus explore how this local event influenced Williams' subsequent poetic development. Such an in-depth exploration of Williams' development will ultimately enhance our understanding of what this poet from Rutherford, New Jersey tried telling the American people about themselves.

A Struggle to Define America

For this study's focus on Williams, the 1913 silk strike's importance concerns four main factors: it drew attention to the industrial history of the city of Paterson; it attracted outside radical groups, like the Industrial Workers of the World (I.W.W.) and the Greenwich Village intellectuals; it demonstrated a large-scale attempt to utilize art in the service of politics, as evident in the "Pageant of the Paterson Strike"; and it brought together two opposing visions of Americanism. This last aspect of the strike—the attempt to define Americanism—stirred the greatest response among both participants and spectators.

As an artist determined to cultivate his American origins, Williams was undoubtedly drawn to the unique industrial past of Paterson. In explaining his selection of the city for his poem, he writes:

The falls, vocal, seasonally vociferous, associated with many of the

ideas upon which our fiscal colonial policy shaped us through
Alexander Hamilton, interested me profoundly—and what has resulted
therefrom. (A 391)

Alexander Hamilton helped to shape America by his industrial development of the Passaic Falls and Paterson. This fact upset Williams, for he blamed Hamilton's industrial vision and fiscal plans for the problems in American society. He believed the industrialization and capitalism that Hamilton espoused corrupted the ideal of a pure democracy and prevented individuals from making "contact" with the true nature of the place. The 1913 silk strike, which magnified the socio-economic divisions of the city, therefore dramatized for Williams the social inequality inherent in Hamilton's vision of America. For the remainder of his life, as evident in his life-long development of *Paterson*, Williams worked to overcome such societal division and discover a "redeeming language" that would unify the people with the true nature of their locale.

Technological advances in the silk industry precipitated the 1913 strike, specifically the introduction of a multi-loom system that enabled fewer broad-silk weavers to produce more silk. It did not take long, however, for the strike to take on larger, more abstract social issues, such as the right of workers to organize and to speak out against the exploitation of labor. The strike involved the skilled and unskilled workers from all three areas of the silk industry: ribbon weavers, dyers' helpers, and broad-silk weavers. They had diverse ethnic backgrounds—English, Irish, Northern and Southern Italian, and Polish and German Jews; yet, the strike brought them together. This solidarity was crucial to the strike's success. They all had different motivations for participating in the strike, yet they all shared the desire to gain more control over their lives in America. Historian Steve Golin clearly expresses how this desire motivated the different workers: "As craftsmen and English-speaking Americans, the ribbon weavers were struggling in 1913 to protect a whole way of life; as Italian-speaking proletarians, the dyers' helpers were fighting for a chance to live" (25). Their ability to transcend cultural and occupational differences thus enabled them to consolidate their power and to present a formidable opposition to silk manufacturers.

The I.W.W.'s involvement helped to transform the silk strike. Just off its 1912 woolen strike victory in Lawrence, Massachusetts, the I.W.W. looked to follow up that success with another success in Paterson. Because of its revolutionary reputation, however, the I.W.W. stood as a lightning rod for the regional media and the Paterson authorities. It had a reputation as a violent group of radical terrorists. Aware of their public reputation, the primary leaders of the I.W.W. stressed non-violence during their speeches in Paterson. Nevertheless, much of the media still perceived the I.W.W. as a serious threat to the country. This perception emerges clearly in the following *New York Times* editorial:

> From the time that the Industrial Workers of the World, according to their practice, interested themselves in this strike, it has become a part of the general assault of Socialism upon society, and more immediately of the death grapple between Socialism and organized labor. ("Socialism" 10)

The I.W.W.'s participation in the Paterson silk strike raised the stakes involved in its settlement. It became a fight for Democracy over Socialism, a fight to protect a way of life in America.

Both sides that participated in the strike presented contrasting visions of what it meant to be an American. An example of these stark differences appeared on March 17, 1913, Paterson's official Flag Day. As historian Anne Huber Tripp explains, the silk manufacturers were intent on "transforming the conflict into one in which Americanism was the central issue" (90); consequently, on March 17th, the manufacturers raised American flags over every mill. The striking workers responded to this display by leading their own parade with the following banner:

> We weave the flag.
> We live under the flag.
> We die under the flag.

> But dam'd if we'll starve under the flag. (90)

The contrasting images of the American flags over the manufacturers' mills and the workers' banner illustrate the depth of the struggle occurring in this industrial city. For these people, the meaning of America was being decided. Was it the land of equal opportunity? A democratic country where hard-working individuals prospered? Or, with Catholina Lambert's castle overlooking the mills, was this country little better than the countries they left behind? Answers to such questions were not easy, and many people like Williams spent a lifetime trying to answer them.

Another significant factor in the strike effort were the Greenwich Village intellectuals. John Reed played an especially pivotal role in the strike. His arrest as a "Poet" in Paterson brought media attention to the strike and resulted in his article "War in Paterson," which appeared in *The Masses*. This article portrays the strike as a civil war between workers and Mill Owners who "control absolutely the Police, the Press, the Courts" (26). Reed's work in Paterson had lasting implications; even Williams was affected by the "bright boy." When explaining the choice of Paterson in his *Autobiography*, he remarked "Even today [it is] a fruitful locale for study. I knew of these things. I had heard. I had taken part in some of the incidents that made up the place. I had heard Billy Sunday: I had talked with John Reed [. . .]" (391). That he mentions talking with Reed in explaining his choice of the city of Paterson, written so many years later, is highly significant. Reed's activities in Paterson were influential throughout the artistic community. As Golin contends, "Mainstream writers who were not necessarily moved by the arrest of silk strikers, Wobbly agitators, or even Socialist editor Scott, took an interest in what happened to John Reed. Reed was a kind of bridge in himself" (136).

Reed's major project in Paterson was the "Pageant of the Paterson Strike." He directed over a thousand strikers in the pageant at Madison Square Garden on June 7, 1913. The performance enabled actual strikers to dramatize the story of their hardships on a grand New York stage. According to Steve Golin, it functioned as a way for them "to publicize the dramatic class struggle then taking place in Paterson, in the hope of influencing the outcome" (161). It did gain publicity for the silk strikers, but it also presented an innovative artistic approach for portraying the lives of lower-class Americans. With the strikers presenting their own story, Reed's pageant offered artists, like Williams, a unique artistic expression of modernity. Even more than the radical paintings at the 1913 Armory Show, the pageant may have offered Williams an artistic model rooted in the lives and language of his own locale. Certainly, the "talk" of Reed and Williams further nourished those roots.

The 1913 silk strike thus brought to the surface key issues about patriotism, the role of art in politics, and the social rights of the lower class in America. When the strike officially ended in August, an overwhelming victor failed to emerge. The strikers returned to work without winning any substantial demands. Silk manufacturers had their workers back; however, the industry was changing and the silk could be produced cheaper in Pennsylvania. The I.W.W. left Paterson much weaker than when it entered. Even the Greenwich Village intellectuals abandoned Paterson disillusioned; soon after the Pageant, Reed left with Mabel Dodge for Europe. As for the city itself, it was headed downward. As Tripp contends, the 1913 strike "played a role in the decaying process of the venerable industrial center [. . .] [It] expedited the decline" (241). Paterson's nickname as Silk City soon became outdated; instead it gained "a reputation as a hotbed of revolutionary sentiment which it could not overcome and served to repel industries which might have taken the place of silk" (241). Certainly, Paterson was a changed place following the 1913 strike.

Williams Saw the Significance

Williams did not miss the socio-historical significance of the 1913 Paterson silk strike. This tense standoff between capital and labor, in the exact place where Hamilton envisioned America's manufacturing utopia, drew Williams' attention to the history that constituted this place. The strike also re-emphasized to Williams the deep social and economic divisions existing between the people inhabiting this locale. It illustrated to him how far away all Americans were from sharing the American ideals of freedom and equality.

More important, Williams did not miss the artistic value of this event. He did not portray the strike as a romantic rebellion; instead, he saw it as a brutal affair. Yet, despite this brutality, the 1913 silk strike became poetry for Williams. He saw that he could create a distinctively American art by descending downward to the actual circumstances that contributed to the rough experiences of these people and that constituted this local industrialized city. As he ventured towards a revolutionary form of poetry, he desired to return artistically to this place and tell its story in its own language and form. His innovative poem *Paterson* is the culmination of this epic desire. Yet, it must be remembered that the roots of this poetic achievement stretch back to 1913. By examining this year, in particular Paterson's silk strike, we will have a clearer understanding of Williams' poetic development and his purpose in creating *Paterson*.

CHAPTER 1

THE EARLY LIFE AND POETRY OF DR. WILLIAMS

To understand the transformation that William Carlos Williams undergoes as a poet in 1913, it is necessary to examine the poetry he wrote prior to this year. By reviewing this poetry, we will reach a clearer understanding of the poetic changes that "The Wanderer" signals in Williams' work and appreciate the impact of the 1913 silk strike on his poetry. We must also examine Williams' early social and cultural experiences. These experiences illustrate that Williams, though a member of the middle class, came into contact with the lower class and local urban squalor prior to 1913. For the most part, however, his early poems do not reflect these experiences.

Williams spent his childhood in a comfortable home on Passaic Avenue in "respectable" Rutherford, a conservative town known for its staunch Republican affiliation (Frail 17). His father William George was English, and his mother Elena, who was from Puerto Rico, was of mixed ancestry: French, Spanish, and Dutch-Jewish (Whittemore 14). Spanish, English, and some French were spoken in the house and the visits of diverse friends and relatives to Rutherford created a unique linguistic situation for the young William Carlos. According to biographer Paul Mariani, "It was a strange, heady, unorthodox linguistic minestrone Williams tasted growing up" (17).

Williams' father was not "rich." He worked for the company of Lanman and Kemp, which produced a cologne-like product called "Florida Water." Williams claimed that "Pop never in his life made more than the barest possible income on which to support" his familial responsibilities (A 50). The quality and expense of his schooling, however, makes it apparent that Williams did not have the typical educational experiences of a first generation American of his time. During 1897-98 Williams, then fourteen years old, and his younger brother Edgar went off for schooling at the Chateau de Lancy near Geneva, Switzerland. Here they "heard a polyglot of tongues" (Mariani 25). Soon after their year abroad they were sent to the prestigious Horace Mann School in New York City from 1899 to 1901. Following his schooling at Horace Mann, Williams gained direct admission into the Medical School at the University of Pennsylvania; he attended the University from 1902-1906.

Williams held a much different attitude towards America and Europe than his parents. His father never sought American citizenship. He was "really a socialist to a certain extent" (INT 51), as Williams suggested. His mother Elena remained discontent in Rutherford and longed for her romantic Parisian school days. In contrast to his Anglophile father and Francophile mother, Williams embraced his American identity. When his University of Pennsylvania friends Ezra Pound and H. D. left America for Europe, Williams resolutely stayed in his native land. He devoted himself to cultivating his American identity:

> Of mixed ancestry I felt from earliest childhood that America was the only home I could ever possibly call my own. I felt that it was expressly founded for me, personally, and that it must be my first business in life to possess it [. . .] (SL 185)

He believed that in order to create American verse, he needed to live in America and surround himself with the sights and sounds of the place. His determination to write a distinctive American verse was ridiculed by his friend Pound. In a November 1917 letter, Pound writes:

> And America. What the hell do you a bloomin foreigner know
> about the place. [. . .] [Y]ou've never been west of Upper Darby, or
> the Maunchunk   [sic] switchback. [. . .] My dear boy you have
> never felt the woop of the PEEraires. You have never seen the
> projecting and protuberent [sic] Mts. of the Sierra Nevada. WOT
> can you know of the country? (EP/WCW 30-31)

Despite Pound's teasing about his qualifications for writing 'American' poetry, Williams believed in his approach and maintained his desire to create a distinctive cultural verse.

Williams' devotion to his native country was complicated. Increasingly, he became hostile to the European influence over American letters. "Our enemy is Europe," he writes in *The Great American Novel* (1923), "a thing unrelated to us in any way" (I 209-10). Williams' artistic patriotism, however, did not blind him to America's faults. Later on in *The Great American Novel*, he memorably proclaims: "I am saying that America will screw whom it will screw and when and how it will screw" (210). Williams' devotion to America thus involved a cynical understanding of what America could do to a person. He knew that his country promised much but disappointed many. He saw this scenario repeated time and again in the lives of the immigrants and poor he treated as a doctor. He believed that this disappointment was the result of American capitalism and viewed the manipulation of money as a serious threat to America. In a 1960 interview he declared, "Money is the death of America" (INT 51).

Other Worlds Open to the Doctor

A closer look into Williams' early experiences as a doctor offers further insight into his perception of America. Working as a physician put him into direct contact with people from a lower socio-economic status. These people knew both the hope and disappointment of America. His work thus offered him the chance to see first-hand a different type of American experience.

Williams did not decide to pursue medicine at the University of Pennsylvania at the expense of his poetic pursuits. He made his decision for practical, economic reasons:

> [. . .] it was money that finally decided me. I would continue
> medicine, for I was determined to be a poet; only medicine, a job I
> enjoyed, would make it possible for me to live and write as I
> wanted to. I would live: that first, and write, by God, as *I* wanted
> to if it took me all eternity to accomplish my design. (A 51)

For Williams, medicine and poetry were inextricably intertwined. His work as a doctor brought him into direct contact with places and lives that seemed far removed from the classrooms of Geneva and Horace Mann. Again, in his *Autobiography*, Williams explains the importance of his medical career to his poetry:

> [. . .] my "medicine" was the thing which gained me entrance to
> these secret gardens of the self. [. . .] I was permitted by my
> medical badge to follow the poor, defeated body into those gulfs
> and grottos. And the astonishing thing is that at such times and in
> such places—foul as they may be with the stinking ischio-rectal
> abscesses of our comings and goings—just there, the thing, in all
> its greatest beauty, may for a moment be freed to fly for a moment
> guiltily about the room. (288-289)

Williams' work thus allowed him to know people in the most intimate and vulnerable ways. He continually tried expressing in his verse the "beauty" of the "thing" that he discovered through this personal contact with his patients.

Upon graduating from medical school in 1908, Williams interned in New York City. He started out at an old French hospital on Thirty-Fourth Street, between Ninth and Tenth Avenues (A 71). Again, he integrated himself into a diverse linguistic environment. Mariani comments,

> The French Hospital was, as its name suggested, run by French-

speaking Sisters of Charity, and cared for the French- and Spanish-speaking immigrants living on New York's Lower West Side at the turn of the century. (42)

Interning at this hospital afforded Williams the chance to experience and to observe city life. Williams recounts a variety of patients. In particular, he remembers a "poor whore" whose "breasts were especially lacerated and on one could be seen the deeply imbedded marks of teeth, as if some animal had attempted to tear the tissues away" (A 81). He also recalls a sandblast victim from the excavation of Pennsylvania Station who wore "a woman's silk chemise with little ribbons at his nipples [. . .]" (82). No doubt, as these recollections illustrate, Williams gained further education in the city, an education consisting of darker lessons about the cruelties and perversities tucked away from "respectable" folks.

His next medical assignment was a year at the Nursery and Child's Hospital in Hell's Kitchen, which was known at that time as "San Juan Hill." Such a move to this "notorious" neighborhood illustrates a determination on Williams' part, or perhaps a curiosity, to enter a geographically close locale that was socially far removed. As Williams recalls, "We didn't go out much after dark unaccompanied, man or woman. There were shootings and near riots and worse practically every week-end" (A 93). No doubt Hell's Kitchen put Williams in contact with many of the elements contributing to America's social unrest—poverty, worker exploitation, and class divisions. This section of the city also educated him about how living itself can be a daily challenge. Williams labels the female patients at this hospital "the dregs of the city, a fine crew" (94). The children were more of the same to Williams. When Viola Baxter visited and reprimanded Williams for not immediately changing a baby's diaper, he responded:

You ought to have seen this brat when we got him. He was the most bedraggled, neglected, dirty, emaciated piece of garbage—you couldn't possibly imagine what he looked like—sores, rickets, his legs out of shape, and look at him now—he's beautiful! (A 96) Typical Williams. He could callously describe a child but also find a beauty in the child's crudeness. That is why he could describe the female patients at the hospital as both "dregs" and a "fine crew." He perceived a crudeness and beauty in these people's lives and cherished this discovery.

Williams heard the sounds of pistol shots, the screams of morphine addicts, and the cries of discarded infants during his internship in Hell's Kitchen. One experience that vividly stands out for him from this time period is the bureaucratic corruption in the hospital. Williams tells how he was asked as Resident Surgeon to sign some official forms about the business of the hospital for January of 1909. Williams asked to see how the figures were derived, but his request was denied. He refused to sign the report and was suspended for two weeks. He later resigned from the hospital. Eventually he found out that it was a petty graft scheme. This greedy corruption of the system angered Williams and stayed with him for some time: "To hell with them all, I thought" (A 105). Following these very intense New York experiences, Williams' father paid for him to study abroad in Leipzig. When he returned to America in 1910, he returned to Rutherford and established his own medical practice in his parents' home.

This brief biographical synopsis of Williams' early medical experiences shows his exposure to the brutality of slum life. As with all of his other contacts with his coarse surroundings, Williams was unable or unwilling to write poetry about these things. Not until his 1914 poem "The Wanderer," with its striking, starving mill workers and the polluted Passaic, could Williams represent his locality in his poetry.

Williams' Early Poetry: Imitation and Variation

Prior to the 1913 silk strike and the publication of "The Wanderer," William Carlos Williams seriously committed himself to writing poetry. In his *Autobiography*, he recalls that he began writing poetry during a depressed period in 1901 when for health reasons he was ordered to stop participating on the track team (46-47). He then presents his first poem:

> A black, black cloud
>
> flew over the sun
>
> driven by fierce flying
>
> rain. (47)

Initially Williams felt overjoyed by his creation. However, he was not sentimentally blinded to its artistic merit; he found the logic of the poem, the rain driving the clouds, "stupid." Creating the poem, however, helped to raise his spirits. He wrote, "the joy remained. From that moment I was a poet" (47). This short poem foreshadows some of the qualities of Williams' later work. For example, the concentrated image, enjambment, and unrhymed lines look forward to his later stylistic characteristics.

Following 1901, Williams committed himself to becoming a "great" poet. His early productivity, however, involved a unique poetic division. He created a public and a private poetry. The first followed the dictums and traditional models found in his standard school anthologies. The second style of poetry he wrote in a series of notebooks. (Nobody is sure of the exact number or the precise location of these notebooks.) Williams explains that he used these notebooks for "Whitmanesque 'thoughts,' a sort of purgation and confessional, to clear my head and my heart from turgid obsessions" (A 53). In discussing these notebooks' significance, Mariani suggests that they offered Williams a place where he "could put down his free-ranging, derivative Whitmanesque thoughts, since it was Whitman of all the poets he had so far read who first made him aware of what was new in American poetry" (31). An examination of these mystery notebooks would no doubt enable a more thorough analysis of Williams' early poetic development. Yet the existence of such notebooks, whether read or unread, tells us that Williams had a place, albeit unknown and private, where he unloosened his thoughts and felt free to create experimental verse. Having such a space while generating imitative, traditional poetry no doubt nurtured both his determination to develop his own unique style and his desire to help create a "different" type of poetry.

Before examining Williams' early published poetry, we should first consider Williams' "secret epic" (Mariani 53). Williams began this poem during his final year at the University of Pennsylvania and continued to work on it for the next three years during his New York hospital period; he never completed or titled it. Despite his gritty city experiences, Williams set his romance in the medieval period. The poem concerns a king, Don Pedro of Navarre, trying to poison his son Philip following Philip's wedding to Oradie. As the story develops, the king poisons everyone at the feast, including himself, in order to kill his son. The son survives this mass murder because a devoted old nurse gives him an antidote before her own death. When Philip awakens, he finds himself in a new place with a strange language. According to Williams, the young prince then wanders through the land attempting to piece together his vague remembrances of his former life. Williams writes, "So he went on, homeward or seeking a home that was his own, all this through a 'foreign' country whose language was barbarous" A 60).

Williams uses blank verse and a stilted language throughout the poem. Here is the opening:

> When chivalry like summer's crimson fruit
> From blossom, April's flimsy pride and all
> The ripening seasons, burst at length full frocked
> Resplendent on her prime, when kings were young
> And liegemen bold ambitious and full oft
> Of equal blood with sovran lived a knight
> Don Pedro was he clept, prince of Navarre. [. . .]
> (qtd. in Fisher-Wirth 66)

According to Ann Fisher-Wirth, "It is awkwardly written, shamelessly poetical, and hopelessly derivative [. . .]" (66). Mariani finds it hard to believe "that this man who was stitching up ugly knife wounds and delivering babies of every color and description as the poor mothers came in off the streets for help" was writing "his own initiatory epic, his own version of Keats in this stilted manner" (54).

Williams' imitative tendencies appear throughout both the plot and poetics. In the *Autobiography*, he admits that he turned to Keats, Spenser, and Shakespeare while writing the poem. In this context, Fisher-Wirth suggests that "[i]f the prince in 'Philip and Oradie' [her title] is doomed after his awakening by the absence of a true language, Williams as a poet is doomed throughout 'Philip and Oradie' by the presence of a false language" (83). Williams claims to have tossed this poem with "disgust" into the furnace (A 60). He also links this poem to "The Wanderer" and *Paterson*. After recounting the poem's fiery destruction, he states: "*The Wanderer*, featuring my grandmother, the river, the Passaic River, took its place—my first 'long' poem, which in turn led to *Paterson*" (60-61). Williams' conflation of the events, the burning of his "heroics" and the creation of "The Wanderer," suggests that for Williams this act of destruction cleared the way for his more innovative creations. Fisher-Wirth contends that Williams understood that his poem was a failure and that was why he destroyed it. She suggests, "Had he not done so, had he held on to 'Philip and Oradie,' there would never have been what we know as William Carlos Williams" (81).

Williams did not publish his first book of poems until 1909; Reid Howell, a local Rutherford printer, printed the book at Williams' expense. *Poems* encapsulates Williams early imitative tendencies. The titles of these poems indicate their traditional subject matter: "Innocence," "To Simplicity," "The Quest of Happiness," "The Loneliness of Life," "To A Lady," "The Bewilderment of Youth," and "Hymn to the Spirit of Fraternal Love." These poems exhibit Williams' imitation of the traditional verse he found in Palgrave's *Golden Treasury*. Not surprisingly, his collection was well-received by a reviewer in his local community paper, the *Rutherford American*: "At odd moments Dr. Williams, one of the bright young men of whom Rutherford is justly proud, has wooed the muse to good effect, and the result is highly creditable" (qtd. in Wallace 8). Ezra Pound reacted quite differently to his friend's first book:

> I hope to God you have no feelings if you have, burn this *before*
> reading. [. . .] Individual, original it is not. Great art it is not.
> Poetic it is. [. . .] There are fine lines in it but nowhere I think do
> you add anything to the poets you have used as models. [. . .] you
> are out of touch. –that's all— (EP/WCW 14-15)

To understand Pound's criticism of Williams' book, one needs to look at the poetry itself. Here is a poem dedicated to H. D. entitled "The Uses of Poetry":

> I've fond anticipation of a day
> O'erfilled with pure diversion presently,
> For I must read a lady poesy
> The while we glide by many a leafy bay,
>
> Hid deep in rushes, where at random play
> The glossy black winged May-flies, or whence flee
> Hush-throated nestlings in alarm,
> Whom we have idly frighted with our boat's long sway.
>
> For, lest o'ersaddened by such woes as spring
> To rural peace from our meek onward trend,
> What else more fit? We'll draw the light latch-string
>
> And close the door of sense; then satiate wend,
> On poesy's transforming giant wing,
> To worlds afar whose fruits all anguish mend. (CP1 21)

Technically, this poem illustrates Williams' standard, unimpressive use of the sonnet form. "The poems should be classified as sonnets," he later admitted, "not the Shakespearian sonnet, but the sonnets of Keats and other romantic poets" (IWWP 10). In this particular sonnet, Williams uses a standard rhyme and meter and a stilted, artificial sounding language complete with such un-Williams-like phrases as "lest o'ersaddened by such woes as spring." Also, the poet's transcendence to an Edenic world of fruitful pleasure seems worlds away from the places that Williams takes us to in his later poetry.

Another poem entitled "Love" also offers a representation of the poetry Williams wrote during his New York City years. This twelve-line poem expresses the passion and pain of love. The first and third quatrains are the same:

> Love is twain, it is not single,
>
> Gold and silver mixed in one,
>
> Passion 'tis and pain which mingle
>
> Glist'ring then for aye undone. (CP1 21)

Again, Williams tries hard to sound like a poet with his use of an alternating rhyme scheme and his choice of such archaisms as "twain," "tis," and "aye." The second stanza attempts to clarify his definition of love. If love is just pain, it is "wondering pity"; if it is just passion, it is "foul and gritty." Neither of these feelings has value without the other. Only in his later poetry does Williams see the worth of things that are foul and gritty. *Poems* did not bring Williams poetic fame. According to Williams, "About four copies were sold. I gave others away" (IWWP 10). James Breslin contends that

> the poet who emerges from this collection is one who is entirely
>
> dependent—dependent emotionally upon the remote and lofty
>
> figure of his mother as a mythical female ideal and dependent
>
> artistically upon Keats and the Elizabethans. (11)

Breslin's estimation of Williams' poetic timidity at this time highlights Williams' incapacity to move beyond his British models, even after he has observed the beaten whore, the cross-dressing sandblast victim, and the countless discarded babies. Rod Townley suggests why this is the case:

> Later in life, Williams was to see his poetry and his medical
> practice as nourishing each other; but in his anguished youth (a
> 'hell of repression' as he called it) they seemed irreconcilable, and
> in each he found a refuge from the other. (42-43)

At this time Williams consciously kept his poetry distant from his own local experience. He would draw the latch-string tightly on that "door of sense" to facilitate an imaginary voyage "To worlds afar whose fruits all anguish mend." Williams' conscious decision to separate the poetic self from the real self results in imitative, artificial verse.

There are signs in this 1909 volume of Williams' later poetry. Perhaps the most apparent example is "A Street Market, N.Y., 1908." The title itself refers to a contemporary time and place. This poem illustrates, more than any of his other early poems, Williams' use of his immediate surroundings in his verse. He depicts a scene of American commerce that does not divide diverse people, but brings them together to sing their timeless songs. He expresses this scene, however, in standard rhyme and meter; he also exerts tremendous control over the representation of these people. Stanley Scott Blair contends that Williams has his "far tribes" speak a language they could never understand. He goes on to state:

> But that language could have been easily understood by that "near
> tribe" that constituted the most desirable market for Williams's
> poetic and medical talents: magazine-reading, old-stock, upper-
> class, WASP Americans, who would have agreed heartily with the
> poem's efforts to standardize and to control the mingling, seething,
> immigrant horde. (264-265)

Although he has yet to move beyond poetic conventions, his attempt to represent the lower class immigrants in his verse is significant. This serves as another marker in Williams' development; it expresses his desire to represent the modern local scene.

Uncertain Steps Towards "The Wanderer"

Williams continued to keep his artistic efforts apart from his actual experiences as a physician in Rutherford up through his second published collection entitled *The Tempers*. "There is a big jump," Williams claims, "from the first book to the poems in *The Tempers*. The lines still begin with capitals in *The Tempers*, and there is rhyming very definitely, but the rhyme schemes are quite complicated [. . .]" (IWWP 15). "Peace on Earth," for example, illustrates this "complicated" rhyme scheme. Here is the poem's final stanza:

> The Sisters lie
>
> With their arms intertwining;
>
> Gold against blue
>
> Their hair is shining!
>
> The Serpent writhes!
>
> Orion is listening!
>
> Gold against blue
>
> His sword is glistening!
>
> Sleep!
>
> There is hunting in heaven—
>
> Sleep safe till tomorrow. (CP1 3)

There is certainly metrical and rhythmical variation here. Williams also displays an effort to experiment with stanzaic patterns; he has departed from his use of the sonnet form. However, he is still trying to sound like a "poet." This pose is evident in the references to Orion's heavenly hunt, the refrain "Gold against blue," and the numerous exclamation points. Despite some variations, these conventional poetic devices continue to reflect this poem's imitative quality.

Another poem, "First Praise," seems all the more imitative and artificial. Lines like "Thou art my Lady" and "I have lain by thee on the brown forest floor" sound stilted and dated; one wonders aloud, can this be the same poet who would later write of the "Beautiful Thing" in *Paterson*? As Williams recalls in regard to this poem,

> I should have written about things around me, but I didn't know
> how. [. . .] I was just on the verge of saying right, but I couldn't
> get it out. I knew nothing of language except what I'd heard in
> Keats or the Pre-Raphaelite Brotherhood. (CP1 473)

This self-criticism could also be leveled against the poem "Postlude," which demonstrates Williams' poetic distance from the local subject matter surrounding him.

> Your hair is my Carthage
> And my arms the bow,
> And our words arrows
> To shoot the stars
> Who from that misty sea
> Swarm to destroy us. (CP1 4)

His references to Philae and Poseidon and metaphors/ similes associated with Carthage, Venus, and Mars illustrate his mind-set that to write poetry required classical allusions. This conscious effort to sound "poetic" caused him to overlook a unique expression of his modern world.

In "The Fool's Song," Williams again tries to fit himself into a poetic tradition—this time he speaks as the wise fool. This imitative sing-song verse reflects Williams' exhaustion of conventional poetic language. It is inadequate for expressing the "beauty" he has glimpsed in those "foul" regions. In the poem, he sings about how he has "tried to put / Truth in a cage," but it broke his "pretty cage" (CP1 5). As Stanley Scott Blair suggests, "All the meters and rhymes in the world could not hold the truths Williams was beginning to see in his daily routine as a physician" (282). If he is to create a truly new American poetry, Williams himself needs to break free from the limitations of his poetic models.

There are distinct signs in *The Tempers* of what is to come from Williams. These signs offer glimpses into the direction that Williams will ultimately pursue.

For instance, here is the poem "Mezzo Forte":

> Take that, damn you; and that!
>
> And here's a rose
>
> To make it right again!
>
> God knows
>
> I'm sorry, Grace; but then,
>
> It's not my fault if you will be a cat. (CP1 7)

The cursing and the subsequent apology to Grace seem a harbinger of Williams' experiments with the American idiom. Breslin notes this "strong feeling expressed in strong speech," but he goes on to argue that it is "a literary convention as old as the Petrarchanism it mocks" (14). Although Breslin places the poem in yet another tradition, the tough-sounding colloquial language offers an early example of Williams' attempt to express the speech-rhythms of his contemporary world. This poem also shows Williams experimenting with line-endings and enjambment to create a startling effect.

The poem "Hic Jacet" also shows Williams breaking away from his imitation of traditional models. It is a poem that Ezra Pound thought "the best of all" in *The Tempers* (CP1 475).

> The coroner's merry little children
>
> Have such twinkling brown eyes.
>
> Their father is not of gay men
>
> And their mother jocular in no wise,
>
> Yet the coroner's merry little children
>
> Laugh so easily.
>
> They laugh because they prosper.
>
> Fruit for them is upon all branches.
>
> Lo! how they jibe at loss, for

> Kind heaven fills their little paunches!
>
> It's the coroner's merry, merry children
>
> Who laugh so easily. (CP1 15-16)

Although he uses a conventional stanzaic formation and rhyme, Williams focuses on a sordid subject. He depicts a shocking observation—the merriment of children amid the death that surrounds them. Williams' use of such a non-traditional subject draws attention to itself in a collection of poetry loaded with classical allusions and traditional themes. Although Rod Townley finds the poem's tone forced, he argues that it "represents a real advance over anything in the first book" (70). He claims that it shows that Williams is "willing to look low instead of high for his subject matter, and that he is able to enjoy situational perversities without indulging in moral judgements."

Finally, there is "Contemporania." This poem embodies Williams' struggle to break from poetic tradition and forge his own distinctly American verse. Breslin classifies this poem as "the most direct tribute to Pound in *The Tempers*, [but it] also asserts Williams's awareness of the fundamental difference between Pound and himself" (15). "Contemporania," as the note for the poem suggests, was most likely a response to Pound's "Salutation the Second," where he claims to have "just come from the country." Pound's poem was one of eleven in which he published in *Poetry* under the general title "Contemporania." The poem which immediately follows "Salutation the Second," "Pax Saturni," ridiculed the state of American poetics and opened with lines from another "contemporary" poet's poem—John Reed's "Sangar." Pound distorted the meaning of Reed's lines to make his point about the poor state of modern poetry.

Williams' "Contemporania" does not use Reed's poem to begin, but it does express Williams' concerns about creating modern verse.

> The corner of a great rain
>
> Steamy with the country

Has fallen upon my garden

I go back and forth now
And the little leaves follow me
Talking of the great rain,
Of branches broken,
And the farmer's curses!

But I go back and forth
In this corner of a garden
And the green shoots follow me
Praising the great rain.

We are not curst together,
The leaves and I,
Framing devices, flower devices
And other ways of peopling
The barren country.
Truly it was a very great rain
That makes the little leaves follow me. (CP1 16)

The poem has both an irregular stanzaic pattern and metrical variation; it also doesn't have a traditional rhyming pattern. In response to Pound's poem, it alludes to the poet's place in the country and his capacity to make his poetry new. The "little leaves" and the "great shoots" follow him as he walks "back and forth." These common images represent the contemplative Williams' internal poetic struggle; it portrays his feelings of connection to past traditions, those "little leaves," and his need to cultivate a new poetry, those "green shoots." Breslin interprets Williams' poem as "praising Pound for his role in breaking up established human and literary orders. [. . .] [T]he Williams of 'Contemporania' rejoices in chaos" (16). The narrator in the poem, however, seems more contemplative of what such flux means, rather than celebratory. He alone remains in the garden to ponder the destruction and creation of this "steamy" force; as the resolute Rutherfordian who refuses to emigrate from this "barren country," he knows he must deal with the complex implications of the rain.

As evident throughout these varied selections, *The Tempers* exhibits Williams' struggle and determination to prove his poetic abilities. Another significant poem from this time period, which Williams did not include in his 1913 collection, is "Sicilian Emigrant's Song." Harriet Monroe published this poem in her June 1913 issue of *Poetry*. In the three-stanza poem, the Sicilian Emigrant sings to his "Donna" about leaving the blue skies of Palermo for the grey skies of America. In addition to his use of a subject rooted in his surroundings—the emigrant's experience—the poem is also significant for its attempt to capture the language of the poem's speaker, an attempt to use the simple language of this common person. As Mariani remarks, "here were these transplanted Sicilians speaking their fresh, vibrant, broken English and he tried—faltering—to capture something of their music [. . .]" (97). To demonstrate this point, here is the poem's second stanza:

> O—eh—li! La—la!
>
>   Donna! Donna!
>
> Grey is the sky of this land.
>
> Grey and green is the water.
>
> I see no trees, dost thou? The wind
>
> Is cold for the big woman there with the candle.
>
>   Hey—la!
>
> Donna! Donna! Maria! (CP1 26)

Regardless of the locale, however, the emigrant's song to his "Donna" will persist.

In the final stanza, he puts down his guitar with the promise that he will "sing thee more songs after the landing." Williams did not include the poem in *The Tempers*, perhaps, as Whittemore suggests because he was unsatisfied with it— "He was not ready for the happened-on yet" (107). Nevertheless, as evident in this poem's speaker and language, Williams' poetic transformation was underway.

At this point in his writing, Williams' poems show hints of his later poetic tendencies—experimentation with form, a desire to express everyday speech rhythms, and a willingness to select sordid subject matter. Yet, what does not appear should also be considered in regard to his poetic development. Williams deliberately kept himself out of *The Tempers* and as a result created, for the most part, conventional poetry. His work as a doctor with people from different ethnic groups and social classes is missing. By reading *The Tempers*, one would not know that a doctor who treated the middle and lower classes surrounding Rutherford wrote this poetry. The collection portrays a young poet practicing his craft. It reflects his ability to write conventional verse and his attempt to develop his own style. In the end, *The Tempers* clearly shows the state of Williams' poetry prior to his creation of "The Wanderer."

CHAPTER 2

THE "DUSTY FIGHT" AND WILLIAMS' "THE WANDERER"

Paterson is a city with a unique history. It was established in the late 1700s and through the nineteenth and early twentieth century it emerged as a leading industrial center. Its industrial focus attracted both skilled and unskilled immigrant labor. First, the English, Irish, and Germans arrived to work in the cotton mills; later the Italians, Poles, and Lithuanians came to work in the silk mills. Different cultures, different languages, and different religions all became part of the Paterson social scene. These diverse people all came to Paterson with a common desire to work toward a better way of life. All too often, however, they came away from their millwork frustrated and disillusioned about the real opportunities available to them. Their discontent led to protests and serious disputes with mill owners and managers. Consequently, the city of Paterson also became known for its labor unrest. The 1913 silk strike, though a significant labor event, was far from the only strike that occurred in Paterson. It was, in fact, one of many strikes. Yet this well-organized and lengthy strike dramatized the frustrations and disillusionment of the working class of the city.

The Early History of Paterson

To appreciate the impact of the 1913 silk strike on Williams, it is first necessary to understand the history of this city. Paterson is inextricably connected to the industrial history of the United States. In fact, the city owes its existence to the industrial vision of one man—Alexander Hamilton. Opposed to the agrarian ideal espoused by Thomas Jefferson and others, Hamilton believed that the country's future financial growth and stability depended on its ability to break from an exclusively agrarian-based economy and develop manufacturing. As the Secretary of the Treasury under President Washington, he presented his "Report on the Subject of Manufacturers" to the House of Representatives on December 5, 1791. This report highlights Hamilton's conviction about the importance of industrial development to the emerging nation; it also calls for the federal government to assist these industrial ventures with financial support. He believed that his proposal would balance the economy, increase jobs, and attract workers from other nations. In closing, he states that "[t]he measures [. . .] which have been submitted, taken aggregately, will, for a long time to come, rather augment than decrease the public revenue. [. . .]" (337).

Hamilton shared his industrial vision with others in the new nation. Along with several wealthy investors, Hamilton established the Society for the Encouragement of Useful Manufactures (S.U.M.) in 1791. As an officer in the Continental Army during the Revolutionary War, Hamilton had served throughout the state of New Jersey and was familiar with the Passaic Falls. He understood the potential industrial power that this natural wonder could supply if properly harnessed. Not too surprisingly, S.U.M. chose the Passaic Falls as the place to build a model industrial town. Forrest McDonald, one of Hamilton's biographers, points out that this site

> had an abundance of cheap and easily tapped water power at the falls of the Passaic; it was thickly settled and had access to cheap provisions and raw materials; [. . .] It was unnecessary for

Hamilton to add that, being located between New York and Philadelphia, New Jersey was well situated for attracting investors in those two cities. (231-232)

S.U.M.'s plan for the Passaic Falls also required a corporation charter from the state. William Paterson, governor of New Jersey, helped S.U.M. attain the charter by guiding legislation through the state legislature. In recognition of his help, the newly established town was named for him.

Hamilton wanted to construct his city around the textile industry. He looked to England for his industrial model, especially in regard to its use of machinery. In commenting on England's industrial power in his report, he references the English cotton mill. He writes, "The prodigious affect of such a Machine is easily conceived. To this invention is to be attributed essentially the immense progress, which has been so suddenly made in Great Britain, in the various fabrics of Cotton" (252). Hamilton wanted to do more of the same in the United States. To make S.U.M.'s industrial venture successful, Hamilton wanted to import the latest machinery from abroad, as well as the best skilled workers to operate these machines (Miller 301). As John Miller remarks, "another Manchester or Birmingham was to arise on the banks of the Passaic" (300).

Although S.U.M.'s venture seemed destined for greatness, failures and setbacks were more common than successes. In 1792 S.U.M. itself was in danger of financial ruin as a result of a stock market collapse and the inappropriate business dealings of the governor of the Society, William Durer. Pierre Charles L'Enfant, the designer of Washington D.C., was commissioned to plan the new town, but within a year he was replaced by Peter Colt. It was not until June 1794 that the first water-powered factory spun cotton in this location (Scranton 2). Even so, S.U.M's industrial project was in trouble. As Miller explains,

> Lack of capital, frequent changes of plan, the indifference shown by wealthy men to manufactures in comparison with less risky forms of capital investment, and the Society's inability to bring

enough foreign artisans to Paterson cast a pall upon the undertaking. (309)

All of these problems took their toll. By 1797 S.U.M. had abandoned plans for the town of Paterson.

Although Miller claims that Paterson became a "ghost town" following S.U.M's abandonment (310), it did not remain so for long. Members of Colt's family bought S.U.M.'s shares of stock and sought to lease the Passaic Falls' power (Scranton 2). Like Hamilton before them, other manufacturers saw the industrial potential of this place. Eventually, as the finances of the nation strengthened, new mills were constructed. Philip Scranton attributes this construction to national events like Jefferson's 1807 embargo and the war of 1812 (2). Although Paterson experienced its share of economic downturns, for the most part, it continued to grow as a manufacturing center. By 1860 it had become a city that manufactured cotton and silks, as well as locomotives.

A major feature in Paterson's manufacturing history is silk production. Christopher Colt produced silk as early as 1830, but its production lasted only a few months (Scranton 3). It was not until 1840 that John Ryle, an immigrant silk worker from England, showed that this product could be profitably produced in Paterson. By 1860 six silk companies operated in the city and employed six hundred workers (3). A major jump in silk production occurred following the Civil War. By the year 1900, 175 companies and more than 20,000 workers comprised the silk industry in Paterson (4). The city gained an international reputation as "The Lyons of America," referring to the French town known for its silk production. It also gained the nickname "Silk City." Ironically, this industrial city in northern New Jersey, with its poor immigrant population, gained an international reputation for the production of a luxury item like silk.

Along with the rise of manufacturing in Paterson following the Civil War, labor tension also increased in the city. "During the last two decades of the nineteenth century," according to Philip J. McLewin, "New Jersey silk workers struck far more often than those in other states" (136). David Goldberg recounts that "strikes occurred so commonly in Paterson that one historian found that 137 walkouts took place between 1887-1900—a total that does not include the small disturbances that took place on a regular basis in the city" (25). After the turn of the century, this form of labor protest continued. McLewin records that "between 1905 and 1913 there were forty-eight strikes in Paterson" (136-137). Paterson workers gained a reputation for their propensity to protest and the city was known as a hotbed for radical militants. Immigrant English weavers were known as troublemakers. In 1880 one manufacturer remarked that this group "are generally a bad set, a very bad set. They are so tainted with a communistic spirit that we prefer to have nothing to do with them" (Golin 18). In the 1890s the city became known as the "international center of Italian anarchism" (26). In fact, in July 1900 a Paterson anarchist assassinated the King of Italy. It is no wonder, then, that "Silk City" also became known as "Red City."

The 1913 Paterson Silk Strike

The 1913 silk strike re-emphasized the city's radical reputation. The strike was precipitated by workers' fears that they were being replaced by machinery. Prior to 1913, the silk manufacturer Henry Doherty attempted to force his broad-silk weavers to use a four-loom machine instead of the traditional loom machine. Other silk locations in Pennsylvania, with less resistant workers, already used three and four-loom machines. Paterson silk workers, however, saw this technological innovation as a threat to their livelihoods. Anne Huber Tripp interprets the deeper significance of this change:

> In addition to the potential displacement of men by machines, one weaver possibly doing the work of four, the introduction of the multiple-loom system threatened to alter the nature of the entire Paterson silk industry. (45)

Besides the technological changes, another significant issue for the silk workers was the institution of an eight-hour workday.

Rumblings of the impending strike were evident in the unrest at Doherty's mill. On January 23, 1913, approximately 800 broad silk weavers from the mill left their looms (Tripp 64). After only a few hours, Doherty company officials worked out a settlement with the strikers. They agreed to limit a weaver's responsibility to two looms; they added, however, that if a general agreement regarding the loom issue was not worked out industry-wide in thirty days, they would impose the multi-loom system. By January 27, Doherty still had not removed the four-loom assignments and the workers went out on strike again. Workers in a few other shops followed the Doherty workers and also went out on strike. As the stalemate continued, Local 152 of the I.W.W. voted on February 18th to hold a general strike. Then, at 8:00 a.m. on February 25th, several thousand silk workers walked off the job and the 1913 silk strike was underway.

The first day of the strike was crucial. Between 4,000 and 5,000 workers left their positions in the mills. Many of the strikers marched over to Turn Hall to hear speeches from several prominent I.W.W. figures—Carlo Tresca, Elizabeth Gurley Flynn, and Patrick Quinlan. Paterson's Chief of Police, John Bimson, ended this strikers' meeting. He charged the I.W.W. speakers with inciting a riot and arrested them. This type of action foreshadowed the aggressive approach that the Paterson authorities took towards the strike. These early arrests, however, may have had the opposite effect on the strikers than Bimson intended. It seemed to strengthen their solidarity. By February 28th the number of striking workers reportedly increased to 8,500 (Tripp 71). This increase in strikers had people questioning the merit of Bimson's swift action. The following excerpt appeared in the Paterson *Evening News* a few weeks after the incident:

> There is a growing sentiment that the police made a mistake in arresting out of town agitators without their having committed any overt act. There is a principal of American citizenship as old as the Republic and as deep-rooted as the American love of liberty, that

the right of free speech and the right of men to gather together peaceably [. . .] is an inalienable one. (qtd. in Tripp 70)

Bimson's actions substantiated the view among many silk workers that certain "principles" and "rights" were not guaranteed to everyone in the city of Paterson.

To last, the general strike needed workers to walkout from all three areas of the silk industry. Occupational boundaries needed to be crossed, as well as language and ethnic lines. Ribbon weavers were primarily English-speaking American citizens, dyers' helpers were primarily Italian immigrants, and broad-silk weavers were primarily Polish-Jewish immigrants. Initially, the strike involved silk weavers, workers who were directly affected by the multiple loom. On March 1st, however, dyers from Weidmann's and the National Silk Dyeing Company joined the picket lines. With the dyers' participation, the strike gained strength and showed manufacturers the industry-wide implications of this walkout. Tripp contends that "[t]he dye shops [. . .] were the key to the success of the general strike movement" (71). Later, on March 4th, the ribbon silk weavers, who were the most highly paid silk workers, also joined the strike. The willingness of these laborers from different ethnic and religious backgrounds to come together highlights the significance of their solidarity in 1913. From past failures, Golin argues, they had learned "that each trade or group within the industry as a whole could advance only if they all joined together, as a class" (36). By March 6th, it was estimated that over 23,900 workers were united in the general strike (Tripp 73).

With the arrest of Tresca, Flynn, and Quinlan, many outsiders held the impression that the I.W.W. led the strike. There is no doubt that the I.W.W. played a critical role in maintaining and organizing the strike. They held meetings, gave speeches, and planned events to capture publicity. Yet this was the strikers' strike. Steve Golin emphasizes this point:

Local militants planned the general strike, organized it, began and controlled it. [. . .] [T]he contribution of the outsiders was minimal. In a sense, their greatest contribution was that they recognized and encouraged the abilities of the silk workers. (41)

The strikers formed an Executive Strike Committee and a somewhat larger Central Strike Committee. These committees made the crucial decisions regarding strike strategy. The I.W.W. recognized this controlling force. As Elizabeth Gurley Flynn recounted after the strike, "The I.W.W. arranged the meetings, conducted the agitation work. But the policies of the strike were determined by that strike committee of the strikers themselves" (216). When asked about his leadership role upon visiting Paterson, Big Bill Haywood retorted: "I'm not the leader. [. . .] The strike has no leaders" ("Who is the leader?" 204). He was then asked who was in charge. He firmly responded: "The strikers."

Wobblies and Intellectuals

With an understanding that the strikers controlled their strike, there is still a need to clarify the I.W.W.'s role. The I.W.W.'s reputation as revolutionists preceded its entrance into Paterson. Morris Schonback remarks that "[t]he very mention of the IWW, or the 'Wobblies,' had a spine-chilling effect on many people of the day" (55). Prior to arriving in Paterson, the I.W.W. had helped woolen workers in Lawrence, Massachusetts emerge victorious in their strike. With success in Lawrence, the I.W.W. looked to strengthen its foothold in the East and viewed Paterson as promising. Tripp asserts:

> With its long history of labor unrest, the marked proclivity of the silk workers to transform grievances into militant action, and the apparent radical inclination of Paterson's working class population, the New Jersey silk center appeared to be a particularly promising site for an I.W.W. strike. (214)

The I.W.W. thus hoped to garner publicity for the silk strikers' cause, as well as gain converts for their own radical philosophy.

The popular I.W.W. leaders during the strike were Carlo Tresca, Elizabeth

Gurley Flynn, and of course Big Bill Haywood. Their speeches roused strikers and appealed to the strikers' sense of solidarity. Tresca was an Italian revolutionary who left Italy to avoid a prison sentence. Golin suggests that he expressed the mood "of Paterson's fighting Italian community" (29). Elizabeth Gurley Flynn was of Irish ancestry and moved both men and women to action with her rousing speeches. Her leadership showed the influential role women could play in the labor movement. Golin describes her importance to the strikers:

> she was an example of what a woman could be. She seemed afraid
> of no one and totally dedicated to the strike and to the IWW. [. . .]
> This woman, more than anyone, was the leader of the Paterson
> strike. (62)

Yet Big Bill Haywood grabbed most of the public attention. This one-eyed western agitator appeared larger than life. He was a straightforward talker who voiced the strikers' resolve. At one point during the strike he exclaimed, "The strikers in this city will stay out until hell freezes over and then fight on the ice to the finish" (Tripp 106). Tripp claims that Haywood acted "more as an inspirational agitator than an effective strike organizer" (80).

Besides the I.W.W., Greenwich Village intellectuals and activists came to Paterson with the hope of helping strikers achieve their goals. In the Village, they had argued over the plight of American workers. Their talk turned into action when they rode the train to Paterson. Major Greenwich Village participants in the strike included Margaret Sanger, John Reed, Max Eastman, John Sloan, Hutchins Hapgood, and Mabel Dodge. In her autobiography, Margaret Sanger commented upon the activities of the Villagers during the silk strike pageant: "I believe that we all had our parts to play. Some had important ones; some were there to lend support to a scene; some were merely voices off stage. Each, whatever his role, was essential. I only walked on, but it had its influence in my future" (85).

Given this study's concern with the significance of John Reed's conversation with William Carlos Williams about the city of Paterson, Reed's activities during the 1913 strike require examination. Reed came to Paterson an aspiring writer and left the city a committed activist. Lincoln Steffens recalls Reed at this time as "a big, growing, happy being" who would wake him up at night to tell him of the "most wonderful thing in the world" (654). The "wonderful" things he described to Steffens ranged from women and plays to strikers and Bill Haywood. Initially, Reed went to Paterson to observe the strike, but when he was asked to move along by a police officer named McCormick, he refused. The officer then took him to court to face Recorder James F. Carroll. His arrest in Paterson was big news, appearing on the front-page of the *New York Times* under the simple headline: "WRITER SENT TO JAIL." The following is the reported conversation:

> "What's your business?" asked the Recorder.
>
> "Poet," answered Reed.
>
> "What's your business here?" the Recorder asked again.
>
> "None; I am a bystander," Reed replied. [. . .]
>
> The Recorder took McCormick's view of the case and sentenced Reed to jail. (1)

Reed's arrest for merely observing the strike provided the Paterson authorities with unwanted publicity. It also encouraged other writers to follow him to Paterson; as Golin contends, "Reed was a kind of bridge in himself" (136).

Reed spent four days in a Passaic County jail. His prison experience opened his eyes to the hardships of lower-class Americans. He met Carlos Tresca, Bill Haywood, and countless strikers. Robert A. Rosenstone, one of Reed's biographers, claims that Reed's contact with the strikers profoundly affected the young writer:

> Immediately Reed fell in love with these Italians, Lithuanians, Poles and Jews, small, dark, tough, boisterous men who cheered the IWW, incessantly sang union songs and fearlessly denounced their jailers. Many had faces scarred and bruised by billy clubs

> [. . .] Yet all were full of fight and ready to return to the picket
> lines. (121)

After visiting him in jail, Eddy Hunt records Reed exclaiming, "Don't get me out. I'm gathering material for an epic" (Rosenstone 126). Although Reed never created his "epic," his jail experience did become the subject of an article he published in the *Masses* in June 1913, entitled "War in Paterson." Reed's article depicted a class war in Paterson waged by the Mill Owners and supported by the local press and city authorities. He recounted the police officers' brutal treatment of strikers. His article showed "which side of this struggle is 'anarchistic' and 'contrary to American ideals'" (26).

Justice for All?

John Reed initially went to Paterson after listening to Big Bill Haywood's account of Valentino Modestino's death, which had occurred on April 17. Modestino was killed on his porch when O'Brien detectives of the Weidmann Silk Dyeing plant fired into the air to control a restless crowd of strikers. Modestino's death and funeral brought the strikers even closer together. On April 22nd the I.W.W. staged a funeral procession through Paterson that included thousands of mourners wearing red carnations or ribbons. The ceremony, according to Tripp, was "orchestrated to have the greatest publicity effect" (110). *The Rutherford Republican*, one of Williams's hometown papers, even printed a photograph of Valentino Modestino's funeral procession, though the paper mistakenly refers to him as Antonio Vischio ("Strikers" 3). Modestino, though a non-union worker, was held up as a martyr for the cause. Reed later staged this scene as part of the pageant in New York City.

The Modestino shooting illustrated the extent of the silk manufacturers' control over the Paterson authorities. Several witnesses identified Joseph Cutherton, one of the O'Brien detectives, as the shooter, but he never stood trial. It prompted State Supreme Court Justice James F. Minturn to ask, "What power is there in this community that is greater than the power of the law?" The answer, according to historian Steve Golin, was "the power of the manufacturers" (79). The strikers confronted a corrupt justice system, but this bias was not new to them.

The trials of the I.W.W. leaders and a socialist newspaper editor further emphasized this judicial bias. As mentioned earlier, Police Chief Bimson arrested Tresca, Flynn, and Quinlan on the first day of the strike. Haywood was arrested when he arrived in Paterson. All spent time in jail, paid their bail, and went about the work of the strike. The Paterson authorities, however, were determined to put them on trial. The trials began on May 7th. A tremendous show of public support greeted the accused outside the courthouse. *The New York Times* reported that

> [t]he strikers hate the police and the crowd around the Court House gave vent to this feeling in boos and hisses whenever the police sought to drive back those who tried to force their way into the building. [. . .] [When Haywood and the others arrived, t]he response was deafening. It seemed as if every person in the great throng was leather-lunged. ("Storm the Court" 1)

Patrick Quinlan was the first I.W.W. leader to be put on trial. Although his case was the weakest, the prosecutor believed that if Quinlan could be convicted, he could convict any of the I.W.W. leaders (Golin 103). Detectives testified that Quinlan had urged strikers to enter other silk shops and forcefully remove workers. The defense argued that Quinlan had not even spoken at Turn Hall; that he had arrived as Bimson's men were breaking-up the meeting. Adolph Lessig, head of Local 152 of the I.W.W., and Elizabeth Gurley Flynn supported this claim, as well as other strikers (Tripp 122). On May 10th, the jury declared that they were hopelessly deadlocked. "They were denounced by the Paterson Press," according to Golin, "as a disgrace to the community" (103).

The prosecutor immediately scheduled a re-trial. Prior to this trial, an act of sabotage occurred on the railroad. Someone piled rocks on the tracks to obstruct a train supposedly carrying strikebreakers. The Paterson authorities blamed the I.W.W.; the I.W.W. vehemently denied the charge and claimed "the manufacturers had staged the incident to discredit the union on the eve of the Quinlan retrial" (Tripp 123). The jury for the second trial heard much the same testimony. The defense added two character witnesses for Quinlan—Reverend Percy Stickney Grant and a prominent New York lawyer, George Gordon Battle. Also, a reporter from the Paterson *Morning Call* testified that Quinlan had not spoken during the Turn Hall meeting. Despite this additional testimony, the jury handed down a guilty verdict on May 14th. The verdict sent shock waves through the city. As Golin remarks, "The Quinlan verdict, which angered the strikers and made them touchy, encouraged the police to be more aggressive. [. . .] [It] gave the police license" (104). The guilty verdict bolstered the perception among strikers that the silk manufacturers carried out their own form of "justice" in Paterson. Quinlan was not sentenced immediately; his sentencing followed the other I.W.W. trials. These trials, however, did not occur until late in June.

Meanwhile, another significant court trial began on June 2 for socialist editor Alexander Scott of the Passaic *Weekly Issue*. Scott was arrested for an editorial he wrote regarding the Paterson police. The *New York Times* reprinted an excerpt of the editorial:

> Paterson was one [sic] famous as the City of the Reds, the home of anarchists. These anarchists talked a whole lot and made some noise, but they never harmed a hair on any one's head. Now Paterson has become infamous as the City of the Blues, the hotbed of brass-buttoned anarchists. These police anarchists, headed by the boss anarchist, Bimson, not only believe in lawlessness, but they practice it. They don't waste words with workingmen—they simply crack their heads. ("Find Editor Guilty" 1)

Scott's trial became known as "one of the quickest in the history of Passaic County." It started at 10 a.m. and by 2 p.m. a jury declared Scott guilty of "hostility to the Government." Judge Klenert then sentenced Scott to a prison term of one to fifteen years, a fine of $250, and held him on a bail of $3,000. Eventually this conviction was overturned. "The higher bench ruled," according to Graham Adams, "that the original trial judge should have quashed the indictment or directed the jury to render a not-guilty verdict" (88). Scott's guilty verdict thus reinforced the impression that American principles like "liberty," "justice," and "free-speech" were not guaranteed to *everyone* in the city. Instead, those who held social prominence and financial power monopolized these rights and determined how others would exercise them.

The "Electric Moments" of June 7, 1913

The high-water mark of the strike occurred soon after the Scott trial. On June 7 the strikers staged "The Pageant of the Paterson Silk Strike" in Madison Square Garden in New York City. The performance enabled strikers to dramatize the story of their hardships on a New York stage. According to Steve Golin, it functioned as a way for them "to publicize the dramatic class struggle then taking place in Paterson, in the hope of influencing the outcome" (161). It did gain publicity, but it also presented an innovative artistic dramatization of lower-class American lives. As art historian Linda Nochlin argues, the pageant, "among other achievements, articulated the hollowness of the symbols of the American Dream of freedom, democracy and prosperity—for the oppressed immigrant workers of Paterson and by implication, for the nation as a whole" (68). Mabel Dodge, John Reed, and Bill Haywood are attributed with conceiving the idea of this pageant. One night in late April these three, along with an eclectic group of writers and artists, gathered together at the apartment of a schoolteacher friend of Haywood's (Golin 159). Haywood informed the group about the strikers' difficulty generating positive publicity for the strike. "Showing" the strike in New York was then suggested; eventually, this developed into the idea of performing a pageant in New York that would portray the worker's plight (159). Through this uncensored medium, strikers could present to the world their story.

John Reed volunteered his time on this project and emerged as the driving force behind its production. Rosenstone contends, "Of a six-man executive committee, he was the most committed, the most active, the one who gave direction to what was otherwise a 'poor, inefficient, disorganized' crowd of individuals who could agree on nothing but the general idea" (127). Haywood introduced Reed to the strikers on May 19th. Reed then spent a portion of almost every day in Paterson. He wrote the script, chose scenes, and directed the workers. He originally intended a pageant of ten scenes; however, financial constraints forced him to reduce it to six scenes (Tripp 143).

Reed worked closely with the strikers. Upton Sinclair fondly recalled Reed during the rehearsals in an old warehouse: "with his shirt sleeves rolled up, shouting through a megaphone, drilling those who were to serve as captains of the mass" (263). The strikers welcomed a chance to tell their story in New York; the pageant preparations provided them with something to do besides standing on the picket lines. Many of the strikers also believed that the performance would raise money needed for striker relief. With a dual expectation of publicity and money, many of them viewed the pageant as the potential turning point for their success.

Following the lead of Reed, 1,500 performers/ strikers marched to the railroad station, boarded a special train, and left for New York City. Upon reaching New York, the strikers marched up Broadway to Madison Square Garden to rehearse and prepare for their 8:30 performance (Tripp 144). Prior to the performance, however, the show was still not sold-out. There was plenty of interest in the pageant, but many of those who desired entry, in particular Paterson strikers, could not afford the admission fee. A quick decision was made that workers would only be charged a quarter for entrance and it turned out that many were allowed in free. Eventually, all seats in the Garden were filled.

Despite the financial troubles of opening night, the setting for the performance was something to behold. On the tower outside the Garden, there was a red electric light that spelled out I.W.W. This highly visible sign served notice to the city of the I.W.W.'s presence. Inside, red banners and sashes covered the Garden. A sign reading "No God, no master" briefly appeared, but Quinlan removed it. He told reporters that it was "an infernal outrage" and claimed that everyone associated with the Paterson strike "repudiates it" ("PATERSON STRIKERS" 2). The *New York Times* reporter noted that no American flags appeared in the Garden; the place was completely covered in I.W.W. emblems. On stage appeared a backdrop painting of a huge silk mill created by Robert Edmond Jones and painted by the artist John Sloan (Wertheim 54).

In the pageant's program, Reed explained the larger purpose of the performance. He announced that

> [t]he Pageant represents a battle between the working class and the capitalist class conducted by the Industrial Workers of the World (I.W.W.), making use of the General Strike as the chief weapon. It is a conflict between two social forces—the force of labor and the force of capital. (210)

Reed's words reveal his willingness to utilize art in the service of the proletariat. He transformed the Paterson strike into an event dramatizing the larger social struggle occurring throughout America. In the context of Williams' development, the importance of this pageant is not so much in Reed's use of art to engage in class warfare, but in Reed's willingness to represent Paterson and its people in an artistic medium. By using actual strikers to tell their story, Reed thus highlighted the inherent artistic potential of Williams' locale.

The performance began with a whistle call signaling the start of a workday. Then, over a thousand performers entered from the side of the stage and down the aisles. As the *New York Times* reporter recounts, "they walked as if they were ill fed" ("PATERSON STRIKERS" 2). The pageant consisted of six scenes: 1) The Mills Alive—The Workers Dead/ The Workers Begin to Think; 2) The Mills Dead—The Workers Alive; 3) The Funeral of Modestino; 4) Mass Meeting at Haledon; 5) May Day/ Sending Away the Children; 6) Strike Meeting in Turn Hall (210). The audience was enthralled with the performance and cheered or booed or sang with the cast. Mabel Dodge recalled the powerful effect of this bond between the performers and the audience:

> for a few electric moments there was a terrible unity between all those people. They were one: the workers who had come to show their comrades what was happening across the river and the workers who had come to see it. I have never felt such a high pulsing vibration in any gathering before or since. (qtd. Kornbluh 202)

It was Reed's political goal to forge a feeling of unity between the performers and the audience. As Eric Homberger argues, "Reed's first significant political act affirmed the solidarity of strikers and the audience" (51).

Historically, the pageant has been viewed as both a failure and a success. According to Elizabeth Gurley Flynn and others, it negatively impacted the strike's success. These critics of the Pageant argue

> that it detracted strikers from the picket line, introduced factionalism based on the jealousy of those who were not performers, crushed morale when the anticipated relief funds proved illusory, and prompted suspicion that the profits had been diverted into the pockets of its creators or the union organizers. (Tripp 230-231)

Steve Golin's in-depth study of the pageant proves, however, that the Pageant accomplished its primary goal of gaining publicity for the Paterson strikers. He contends, "In terms of its original purpose of publicizing the strike, the Pageant was an overwhelming success" (160).

Artistically, the Pageant received widespread praise and acknowledgement for its innovations. The *Independent* claimed "no stage in the country had ever seen a more real dramatic expression of American life—only a part of it, to be sure, but a genuine and significant part of it" (qtd. in Tripp 146). Another review in *Survey* claimed that "[t]he simple movements of this mass of silk workers were inarticulate eloquence" (214). The same night of the Paterson Pageant another pageant occurred in New York City; it celebrated the twentieth anniversary of the Henry Street Settlement. What makes this pageant noteworthy is the fact that a *New York Times* editorial compared and contrasted the two pageants. The writer claimed that the Henry Street pageant had a "wholesome" influence on the city ("Two Pageants" 8). Meanwhile, he interpreted the Paterson pageant as unruly, "promulgating a gospel of discontent." He concludes,

> In the Henry Street celebration the motive was to exalt progress, intellectual development, and the triumph of civilization. In the other the motive was to inspire hatred, to induce violence which may lead to the tearing down of the civil state and the institution of anarchy.

This contrast illustrates how radical the Paterson Pageant was for its time. It presented a much different image of the poor than productions like the Henry Street Pageant. It portrayed American workers who no longer quietly accepted their lower socio-economic status. This pageant gave them a chance to express their frustration and to demand a change in the traditional economic power structure.

The Paterson Pageant's significance as political art has not been diminished throughout the years. Later critics have also applauded Reed's production. Art historian Linda Nochlin, for example, describes it as "an important incident in the history of radical self-consciousness and in the history of public art in this country . . ." (64). In analyzing both its artistic and political dimensions, Nochlin shows how the pageant offered the Paterson strikers an artistic medium that enabled them to tell the story of their experiences in America.

> [I]t was made dramatically clear that the "new citizens" were contributing more than their dances, their songs and their folk

traditions to this country; they were being forced to contribute their health, their hopes, their honor and their children—forced to live lives of wretchedness and squalor in order that WASP capitalist society might flourish. (68)

In this unique drama, the under-class literally showed American artists what American art should be about—the lives of common American workers. Eric Homberger, in fact, contends that Reed's "central innovation" was the strikers' "self-presentation" (51). John Howard Lawson also sees the pageant in terms of its artistic innovations. He claims:

The audience participation, the living-newspaper technique, the working-class point of view, foreshadow the work of Mayakovsky and Meyerhold in the Soviet Union and Brecht and Piscator in Germany, as well as the New Playwrights' Theater in New York and the social drama of the 1930s. (qtd. in Nochlin 67)

Reed's innovative and radical pageant thus highlights the artistic potential inherent in the lives and language of these lower-class Americans.

Although Williams most likely did not attend the performance (Frail 61), the pageant did receive widespread newspaper coverage. Because of his interest in the performing arts, Williams would no doubt find such a performance appealing. After all, he came to believe that the artist should use local materials to recreate the actual. This pageant, with its use of actual strikers to present their story, offered Williams a unique way of representing the "local" in the creation of his own distinct verse.

The Battle Against Hunger

Besides battling the silk manufacturers, strikers also battled the problem of hunger. This problem constantly threatened striker solidarity. According to Golin, "Hunger was the strongest, most constant enemy of the silk strikers—and the one with which they became the most intimate in the course of the struggle"

(49). Serious efforts were made to combat the hunger problem throughout the strike. A General Relief Committee was organized in mid-March, and relief stations were set-up to provide aid to the strikers. Kornbluh recounts that "[t]wo relief stations supplied food to families. A restaurant fed the single men. A grocery and drugstore were opened and run by the workers" (199-200). On the day that the Relief Committee was organized, a Jewish bakery named the Purity Cooperative Company provided strikers with bread (Golin 47). It is estimated that this bakery provided strikers with close to 30,000 loaves per week (48).

Despite this aid, strikers suffered severely through the summer months. "A terrible thing to see tens of thousands of human beings starved into slavery," Upton Sinclair remarks, "held down by policemen's clubs and newspaper slanders" (262). By July 22, relief activities had to be suspended. In increasing numbers, strikers went back to work. Ribbon weavers were the first to break the industry-wide solidarity and settle on a shop-to-shop basis. Soon other strikers returned to work. The strike, though not officially declared over until August 2, was for all intents and purposes finished. As Flynn recounts, the return to the shops "was the stampede of hungry people, people who could no longer think clearly" (224). Manufacturers had been able to hold out longer than the strikers. As Golin concludes, "The strikers succumbed to hunger after five months and returned to work, many under the old conditions. The most effective strategy for the manufacturers was endurance" (187).

The 1913 Silk Strike and the Arts

The 1913 Paterson strike may have ended in a failure for the workers, but their story became an inspiration to many artists. Some writers who participated in the strike used certain episodes from the struggle in their novels: Ernest Poole's *The Harbor* (1915), Harry Kemp's *More Miles* (1926), and Max Eastman's *Venture* (1927). The strike also inspired the creation of several poems. Rose Pastor Stokes published "Paterson" in *The Masses* November 1913 issue. As the following excerpt demonstrates, Stokes understood why the strike failed and also understood the fact that nothing was resolved in the workers' favor:

> You dream that we are weaving what you will?
>
> Take care!
>
> Our fingers do not cease:
>
> We've starved—and lost; but we are weavers
>
> still;
>
> And Hunger's in the mill! [. . .] (89)

Other poets also created verse about the strike. For the September 1913 inaugural issue of *The Glebe*, the proletarian poet and sculptor Adolf Wolff published "On Seeing the Garment Strikers March," "Elizabeth Gurley Flynn," and "The Revolt of the Ragged." Wolff was a frequent visitor to Grantwood (Naumann and Avrich 487), which was also referred to as Ridgefield, an artist's colony that Williams fondly recalled visiting. Man Ray, one of Ridgefield's residents, even recalled in *Self Portrait* Williams' arrival during a gathering that included Max Eastman and Wolff (40).

Considering all of the artistic interest in the silk strike shown by these other artists, it is not surprising that William Carlos Williams also saw the strike as poetic material. As previously shown, prior to 1913 Williams wrote very little poetry based upon the local people and places surrounding his Rutherford home. Yet Williams did write about the 1913 silk strike. Not only was he moved enough by this strike to include it in a poem, but he also placed "Paterson—The Strike" as the central section of "The Wanderer: A Rococo Study." "The Wanderer" replaced his earlier epic effort. He writes, "It is actually a reconstruction from memory of my early Keatsian *Endymion* imitation that I destroyed, burned in a furnace! It is the story of growing up" (IWWP 25-26). "The Wanderer" is a pivotal poem for Williams; he claims that it led to his creation of *Paterson* (A 61). This connection between the two poems further highlights the importance of the Paterson silk strike in Williams' formulation of his modern epic.

Considering the distance of his poetry from his immediate locale, Williams' decision to write about the volatile social turmoil occurring in Paterson is somewhat surprising. What caused him to write about this specific event? The answer to this question is not easy. As mentioned earlier, the strike received considerable media attention in the surrounding newspapers. It also brought together a diverse collection of radicals and artists. John Thirlwall suggests that the strike was "bound to attract a 'sensitive person' to the strikers":

> Joseph Etton, one of the IWW leaders, when searched by the police on suspicion of seditious literature produced a volume of Shelley's poems; [. . .] Carlo Tresca read Browning and Elizabeth Gurley Flynn "adored" Maeterlinck. [. . .] Williams found a double bond with the workers and their leaders [. . .] (260-261)

Thirlwall claims that Williams "had been impressed by the strike" and sensitive to the brutality.

Williams, Reed, and "A Fruitful Locale"

Williams also may have been strongly influenced by the "poet" John Reed and his well-publicized activities in Paterson. As previously stated, Steve Golin believes that many writers used Reed as a bridge to the crisis in Paterson. When explaining his choice of the city in his *Autobiography*, Williams links his selection of the city to a "talk" with John Reed. After so many years, it is highly significant that he mentions talking with Reed while explaining his choice of Paterson for his poem. In fact, Reed and Williams moved in fairly close circles throughout the 1910s.

Besides the city of Paterson, Ezra Pound functions as one of the common links between the two men. In the April 1913 issue of *Poetry* Williams' close friend Pound created a controversy by misrepresenting Reed's poem "Sangar" in his own poem "Pax Saturni." Pound intentionally took the following lines from Reed's poem out of context: "Long past, long past, praise God / In these fair, peaceful, happy days" (8). In failing to account for Reed's irony, Pound sets up his "Contemporary" as a foolish poet out of touch with the times. He instructs such "flatterers" to go to America.

> Say there are no oppressions,
>
> Say it is a time of peace,
>
> Say that labor is pleasant,
>
> Say there are no oppressions.
>
> Speak of the American virtues:
>
> And you will not lack your reward.

In regard to Reed's social activism in America and elsewhere, Pound's irony seems particularly unwarranted. Yet despite the objections to his misuse of Reed's poem, Pound insisted on the inclusion of these lines in his poem. As Ellen Williams contends, it demonstrates Pound's refusal to "admit the existence of competitors" (45).

In *Poetry's* June 1913 issue, the same month he presented the Paterson Pageant and published "War in Paterson," Reed published a letter entitled "A Word to Mr. Pound." Here is a portion of the letter:

> No, Mr. Aggressively Contemporary Pound, here in America very few people indeed believe that these are "fair, peaceful, happy days." [. . .] Perhaps I wrong you, but no one else misunderstood my lines. If your criticism had been one of poetic form, I should have respected it, at any rate. (112-113)

Reed takes issue with Pound's direct attack, but he also acknowledges Pound's poetic expertise.

Undoubtedly, Williams came across Reed's letter. In the same issue, Williams had five poems published: "Peace on Earth," "Sicilian Emigrant's Song," "Postlude," "Proof of Immortality," and "On First Opening the Lyric Year." It was his first magazine publication in America (IWWP 17). With Pound and Reed's public poetic confrontation, Reed emerges as a participant in the discussion over contemporary American poetry. By November of this year, he stands as a fairly credible poet. In this month, *Poetry* announced its awards for the best contributions of the year. W.B. Yeats won first prize for "The Grey Rock"; Vachel Lindsay was awarded second prize for "General William Booth Enters Into Heaven." There were eight honorable mention prizes awarded. Williams did not receive one of these awards; however, John Reed received an honorable mention for "Sangar." In contrast to Williams, Reed was not only active in Paterson and telling the story of this locale, but he was receiving acknowledgement for his poetry.

Since Reed was all over the New York literary scene during this period, Williams could not have avoided him. Most likely, he was familiar with Reed's publication of "War in Paterson." According to Frail, "Williams evidently read the poetry in *The Masses*, if not the rest of the magazine [. . .]" (104). Eventually, Williams even published poetry in this magazine. Mike Weaver links Reed, *The Masses*, and Williams. He suggests that Williams held a "feeling of identification with the socialist old *Masses*, seen largely through the eyes of John Reed [. . .]" (89). He goes on to describe Reed as "the revolutionist who had doubtless brought his ideas to the Grantwood in New Jersey before the First World War." Williams spent a lot of time at Grantwood. It was a place where he could meet with others to share his work and discuss the latest artistic trends. At Grantwood he met Orrick Johns, Man Ray, Robert Carlton Brown, Marcel Duchamp, and Alfred Kreymborg. Williams and Kreymborg became fast friends and worked together to publish the magazine *Others*. Kreymborg even asked Williams to perform in his play *Lima Beans*, which he hoped to stage at the Provincetown Players Theater. Reed, a member of the Players, enabled Kreymborg to present his work there. According to Kreymborg,

> a leading member of the group had threatened to resign if the play
> was not accepted. Thanks to the pugnacity of this individual, Jack
> Reed, a compromise was reached and presented to Krimmie

> [Kreymborg]. If he would undertake producing the play himself,
> with some actors outside the personnel, *Lima Beans* would have a
> place on the third bill of the season. (*Troubadour* 242)

Thanks to Reed, Williams performed in the play in December 1916. Reed, however, missed the performance due to the removal of a kidney (Frail 66). Nevertheless, this incident shows that Williams and Reed also shared an interest in the performing arts of the time. More importantly, it offers a clear example of Reed's direct influence on Williams' life.

In the chapter of his *Autobiography* entitled "Painters and Parties," which includes his memories of the Armory Show and the Grantwood, Williams recalls an encounter with Reed at a party held by Lola Ridge. According to Frail, this meeting between the two men took place "late in the decade" (66). By this point in his life, it is clear that Reed had become more of a political activist than the self-proclaimed poet arrested during the Paterson strike. He even admitted to Max Eastman the trouble of combining politics and art: "You know this class struggle plays hell with your poetry!" (77). Williams' description of Reed seems to emphasize this idea.

> I particularly remember one night when Reed showed up. A
> plump, good-natured guy who had taken the bit in his teeth and
> was heading out. He played with the poem but was not primarily
> interested in writing. [. . .] He looked at us as if he couldn't quite
> make out what we were up to, half-amused, half-puzzled. [. . .]
> [Louise Bryant] too looked to be outward bound along with John
> of Portland, Oregon. Wise man he to get started early. (142)

Despite Reed's several appearances in a magazine like *Poetry*, Williams dismisses Reed as a poet. He portrays Reed as a "player" but also as an outsider to this gathering of "serious" artists. Reed appears confused and uncomfortable about what Williams and the others are "up to." Yet in this passage there also emerges a clear sense that Williams liked Reed, especially Reed's social activism. Based upon his later association in the autobiography between a conversation with Reed and *Paterson*, this encounter may have been the one that contributed to Williams' selection of Paterson for his long poem. At the very least, it shows that John Reed stood out for Williams among these "Painters and Parties." In the future he would not be the "poet" most often associated with this city, but he does appear to be the one "poet" who called Williams' attention to this place and its people.

The Strike and "The Wanderer"

A definite connection exists between Williams, Reed, and Paterson both during the 1913 silk strike and the remainder of the decade. For now, however, the discussion must focus upon 1913 and Williams' poem "The Wanderer." "The Wanderer" has been interpreted as a poem that signals a change in Williams' approach to poetry. Well-renowned Williams critics have highlighted this poem's transitional importance. In his study *Poets of Reality*, J. Hillis Miller argues that this poem "celebrates the homecoming which makes his poetry possible" (287). He argues that Williams moves beyond his ego; consequently, his "resignation puts him beyond romanticism" (287). Richard Macksey agrees; he interprets the poem's closing image of the narrator's immersion in the Passaic River as a ritual marriage that enables him to possess the here-and-now. Referring to Williams' previous effort to create an epic, he writes: "Unlike the earlier Keatsian wanderings, this voyage, in its absolute submission and possession, brings him home" (141). James Breslin also believes this poem signals a change in Williams' poetry:

> The new Williams is brought forth in "The Wanderer" [. . .] In this poem, crucial to any study of his development, Williams examines his personal and poetic development, renounces the dreamy ideality of the aesthete and identifies himself with the "filthy" but generative reality of the here and now. (20-21)

In accordance with the poem's transitional significance, it is necessary to examine what "The Wanderer" reveals about Williams as a poet in 1913. Williams divides his poem into seven sections: "Advent," "Clarity," "Broadway," "Paterson—The Strike," "Abroad," "Soothsay," and "Saint James' Grove." The "Advent" section opens with the poet-narrator's vague recollection of the time he first saw his muse. Williams based this figure upon his grandmother Emily Dickinson Wellcome (IWWP 26). In the poem, he compares her to a young crow springing from the nest. She circles around the forest, continually stretching towards new distances; the poet follows her.

In the next stanza, the scene sharply shifts from the forest to an approaching city. Echoing Walt Whitman's great poem "Crossing Brooklyn Ferry," Williams' young poet-narrator rides a ferry headed towards "the great towers of Manhattan" (CP1 27). While moving towards the imposing towers of this urban setting, he considers the difficulty of expressing his modern world: "How shall I be a mirror to this modernity?" (28). His anxiety reflects Williams' concern over the value of his earlier poetry and his uncertainty about his ability to create modern verse. "The young ferry traveller of Williams' poem is full of self-doubts," Norman Finkelstein writes, "and feels profoundly alienated in the environment that offers Whitman such exhilaration" (236). Immediately after he questions himself, his muse reappears:

> Suddenly I saw her! and she waved me
>
> From the white wet in midst of her playing!
>
> She cried me, "Haia! here I am son!
>
> See how strong my little finger! Can I not swim well?
>
> I can fly too!" and with that a great sea-gull
>
> Went to the left, vanishing with a wild cry.
>
> But in my mind all the persons of godhead
>
> Followed after. (CP1 28)

She enthusiastically calls to him as her son, playfully exhibits her power, and shows-off her versatility by transforming herself into a sea-gull. Her transformative power enthralls him and he again follows her.

The young poet desires a poetic transformation; he has shown in the first section that he is willing to forgo all else. In the "Clarity" section, he leaves the ferry and takes off on an imagined, romantic flight after his muse. His flight provides him with a new perspective of the world; he sees everything surrounding him differently. This vision causes him to exclaim:

> For this day I have at last seen her,
>
> In whom age in age is united—
>
> Indifferent, out of sequence, marvelously!
>
> Saving alone that one sequence
>
> Which is the beauty of all the world, for surely
>
> Either there, in the rolling smoke spheres below us,
>
> Or here with us in the air intercircling,
>
> Certainly somewhere here about us
>
> I know she is revealing these things!" (CP1 28)

Recalling her "circling in the forest," the muse embodies the circular movements around him, "the rolling smoke" and "the air intercircling." She enables him to behold this scene. He proclaims her power and intends to worship her as his queen. He refers to her as "That high wanderer of byways / Walking imperious in beggary" (28-29). His jubilation is due not only to his new perspective of the world, but his knowledge that his muse embodies the age and aesthetics that he desires to represent in his verse. Seeing his muse near the river, the young poet descends towards her and proclaims his peace within her presence.

The muse does not allow his Whitman-like flight to continue. At the opening of the "Broadway" section, she strikes him from behind—her blow brings down the mists from his eyes and he sees "crowds walking." He has made it to Manhattan. The muse is intent on re-adjusting the young poet's outdated perception of the world. As Breslin explains, "she instructs the hero by undermining his lofty aspirations; she humbles and awakens him by forcing him to concentrate upon the immediate rather than the remote" (21). He must complete his crossing from the forest to the city and come into contact with the crowds of Manhattan. Unlike Whitman, he does not see a vibrant Manhattan; rather, he sees these "men as visions" and describes them as "empty" (CP1 29). In his eyes, they lack any true substance. They have "expressionless, animate faces" and "shell-thin bodies." Their wasted figures seem the result of their existence in a chaotic urban world far removed from the tranquility of the forest. The city reduces them to "jostling close above the gutter, / Hasting nowhere!"

After observing the "empty men" of Broadway, the poet takes a closer look at his muse. Simply stated, she is not what he expected:

> I really scented the sweat of her presence
>
> And turning saw her and—fell back sickened!
>
> Ominous, old, painted—
>
> With bright lips and eyes of the street sort—
>
> Her might strapped in by a corset
>
> To give her age youth, [. . .] (29)

Her transformation into a viable commodity on the street, a prostitute, personifies the buying and selling that characterizes this crowd of men. Although she appears crude and vulgar, she represents a part of the modernity that the poet ignores. Her transformation disgusts him. She insists that the poet look upon the men before him:

> Well, do their eyes shine, their clothes fit?
>
> These *live* I tell you. Old men with red cheeks,
>
> Young men in gay suits! See them!
>
> Dogged, quivering, impassive—

Through these men, she attempts to relate her intimate knowledge of the modern urban world. Knowing his desire to be "modern," she asks the poet, "are these the ones you envied?"

The poet fails to heed her command and look at these men; he also fails to answer her question. He claims that if he could create a poem in her honor, he would make these busy "toilers" once again her worshippers. Obviously, he has missed her point. Her response to his homage is less than enthusiastic: "she sniffed upon the words warily—." He takes her silence as an opportunity to continue his pleading. He addresses her as "old harlot of greatest lusting" and as a "crafty prowler / After the youth of all cities" (CP1 30).

> To you, marvelous old queen, give me,
>
> Them and me, always a new marriage
>
> Each hour of the day's high posting,
>
> New grip upon that garment that brushed me
>
> One time on beach, lawn, in forest!
>
> May I be lifted still up and out of terror,
>
> Up from the death living around me!

The poet wants to escape the sordidness and emptiness he perceives in this urban setting. Frail characterizes his appeal as one "for the power to present the Adamic vision of the city he had earlier, and so persuade the urbanites to seek such freshness" (88). To re-create this power he desires a connection to the natural locale of beach, lawn, or forest that suggests the opening scene of the poem. This urban scene terrifies him and he longs to leave the squalor that surrounds him. His muse grants his request—"with the fall of night she led me quietly away" (CP1 30).

At the start of the poem's central section "Paterson—The Strike," the muse has been frustrated by the poet's failure to look directly at his modern world. Determined to make the poet see this world, she leads him from New York City to the city of Paterson during the strike. She has him follow the same path that John Reed and many other Greenwich Village intellectuals took in 1913. When she awakens him at dawn, the "trembling" poet can see that her expressions have changed in relation to this place: "Her old eyes glittering fiercely—" (CP1 30). Her fierce look seems to personify the divisive emotions felt by both sides during the strike. She then orders the poet out into the "deserted streets of Paterson." Young John Reed also encountered the Paterson streets at dawn: "At six o'clock in the morning a light rain was falling. Slate-grey and cold, the streets of Paterson were deserted" ("War" 26). Whereas Reed was jailed with the strikers, the young poet in "The Wanderer" returns to the room and offers no description of what he sees. In contrast to Reed, he has failed to make contact with the strikers and thus remains apart from an immediate experience of the strike.

When the muse appears that night "in rags" (CP1 30), he pleads with her to alter his appearance: "Great Queen, bless me with your tatters! / You are blest! Go on!" His request for such "tatters" is quite telling. It suggests an effort by the poet to enter Paterson dressed as one of the strikers. Adolf Wolff dramatically portrays this tattered look in his poem "The Revolt of the Ragged":

> We who have but rags to wear,
>
> Let us go out on strike
>
> And face the robber-master class
>
> In all our naked might. (69)

In "The Wanderer" therefore, the poet's request shows an effort to make contact with the people that his muse brings him to see; it is an effort he failed to make in the "Broadway" section of the poem. These "tatters" outwardly seem to identify him with the Paterson strikers.

With his new "tatters," the poet enters Paterson a dramatically different man. He is no longer "trembling" and "shivering."

> Hot for savagery,
>
> I went sucking the air! Into the city,
>
> Out again, baffled, on to the mountain!
>
> Back into the city!
>
> Nowhere
>
> The subtle! Everywhere the electric! (CP1 30-31)

Like the young Reed who went to Paterson to gain a better understanding of the strike, the poet passionately searches for the meaning of this conflict. He does not have a clear direction where to go; he charges back-and-forth between the city and Garret Mountain. Everywhere he wanders, however, he is filled with the electricity of the strike. This electric feeling echoes the type of electricity that Dodge experienced while watching the "terrible unity" of the strikers in the Pageant. A power and energy pervades this place. When the poet moves closer to the source of this electricity, he finds strikers patiently waiting for food:

> A short bread-line before a hitherto empty tea shop:
>
> No questions—all stood patiently,
>
> Dominated by one idea: something
>
> That carried them as they are always wanting to be carried,
>
> But what is it, I asked those nearest me,
>
> This thing heretofore unobtainable
>
> That they seem so clever to have put on now? (CP1 31)

Williams chooses not to depict these strikers in a meeting at Turn Hall or on a picket line outside a mill. He selects a bread-line, a place where the strikers' resolve is most apparent and their solidarity is most vulnerable. Williams also chooses not to depict an unruly mob clamoring for food. Instead, he portrays a patient, orderly, and determined group of protestors. This image conveys the collective force of their action. It leaves the poet questioning how they have achieved this strength of purpose.

Despite this section's strike references, David Frail contends that "very little" of the strike makes it into this poem (89). He interprets this bread-line scene as something Williams "more likely witnessed in the winter of 1913-14, a time of severe unemployment and hunger—and bread lines that did not stand patiently, as does Williams's" (89). Frail's reading, however, discounts the central problem facing the strikers—hunger. As explained earlier, this problem contributed to the strike's failure, despite the extensive relief efforts to provide strikers with food. Frail's interpretation thus devalues the strikers' significance for

Williams. He argues that Williams displaces the political ramifications of this scene. "When he describes the people in the bread line," Frail argues, "he asserts that the quest for beauty is the poet's primary social responsibility" (89). However, this politically charged image of organized strikers reveals Williams' desire to represent the volatile social divisions inherent in this place. He is curious about the "idea" behind their action and seeks to understand the social conditions that have precipitated the strike. He has difficulty understanding them and appears to adopt the popular depiction of the I.W.W. leaders controlling the strike. After all, the people in line are "[d]ominated by one idea" and "always wanting to be carried" (CP1 31).

Again like Reed in "War in Paterson," the poet questions the strikers about their purpose. These men are receptive to Reed: "'Too bad you get in jail,' they said, sympathetically. 'We tell you ever't'ing. You ask. We tell you. Yes. Yes. You good feller'" (30). Unlike Reed, however, the young poet in "The Wanderer" gets no direct answers. The strikers on line remain silent. Despite his "tatters," his sympathy for these strikers, the poet fails to express their speech in his verse. Besides their obvious sense of social dislocation, these strikers also appear to be separated from the poet as a result of an inadequate language. The young poet then works to comprehend the idea behind their solidarity:

> Why since I have failed them can it be anything
>
> But their own brood? Can it be anything but brutality?
>
> On that at least they're united! That at least
>
> Is their bean soup, their calm bread and a few luxuries! (CP1 31)

The poet realizes that he has failed to express their lives and language in his poetry. He has failed to see the poetic potential of his locale. Now, however, he has come to Paterson and perceives the brutality that shapes and unifies them.

As discussed earlier, brutality was evident throughout the strike. Reed emphasized the brutality of Paterson police officers both in "War in Paterson" and the pageant program. In "War in Paterson," he begins by describing how the police, which he calls the servants of the Mill Owners, "club unresisting men and women and ride down law-abiding crowds on horse-back" (26). After his own account of police brutality during the strike, Thirlwall remarks that it is "[n]o wonder" that Williams came to his realization about brutality in "The Wanderer" (260). This brutality shaped the strikers' American experience. It also precipitated their response to stand together and oppose the silk manufacturers and Paterson authorities.

The poet's perception of this crowd brings him closer to this scene. He is changed by what he observes:

> But in me more sensitive, marvelous old queen,
>
> It sank deep into the blood, that I rose upon
>
> The tense air enjoying the dusty fight! (CP1 31)

Interestingly, Ernest Poole describes a similar sensation in his novel *The Harbor*: "I felt myself sink deeper and deeper into the crowd, into surging multitudes of men—till something that I found down there lifted me up and swept me on—into a strange new harbor" (304). The revolutionary power of the crowd seems to carry both men to a new perspective. Williams describes his own response as the "reaction of a sensitive person to the show of force" (Thirlwall 259). Frail argues that Williams views "the strikers in the light of his concern to find beauty and delicacy, not in the light of their concern for economic justice" (89). The poet, however, immerses himself in the divisiveness and explosiveness that constitutes the strikers' fight for economic justice. This immersion changes him as a poet. Thirlwall, using quotes from Williams, clarifies the scene's significance:

> This observation of the Paterson silk strikers on a bread line, who "couldn't get what they wanted," because "The ruling classes relied on force," points up a revolutionary change in Williams' attitude toward poetry. Leaving the romantic foliage of "faery lands forlorn," [. . .] he set his sights on the lives and activities of the people around him [. . .] (259)

Williams momentarily steps away from a distant middle class perspective of the conflict and revels in the revolutionary force that combats the dominant socioeconomic structure.

Although he perceives their revolutionary force, Williams does not romanticize these strikers. He seems unable or unwilling to move beyond his own prejudices of them. He relies on ethnic and class stereotypes. He remarks, for example, "Heavy wrought drink were the low foreheads" (CP1 31). He then goes on to describe the strikers' faces:

> Faces all knotted up like burls on oaks,
>
> Grasping, fox snouted, thick lipped,
>
> Sagging breasts and protruding stomachs,
>
> Rasping voices, filthy habits with the hands.
>
> Nowhere you! Everywhere the electric! (31)

Although the poet wants to know these strikers, he portrays them in crude class terms. Martin Green suggests that these lines indicate "how conservative, indeed crude, his class sensibility was" (231). Williams cannot shake off his prejudicial class perceptions. He is both captivated and repulsed by these protesting laborers.

Like Williams, Reed also focuses on the strikers' faces in "War in Paterson." He observes the following upon entering the County Jail:

> Faces deadened and dulled with grinding routine in the sunless mills glowed with hope and understanding. Faces scarred and bruised from policeman's clubs grinned eagerly at the thought of going back on the picket-line. And there were other faces, too— lined and sunken with the slow starvation of a nine weeks' poverty—shadowed with the sight of so much suffering, or the hopeless brutality of the police—and there were those who had seen Modestino Valentino shot to death by a private detective. But not one showed discouragement; not one a sign of faltering or of fear. As one little Italian said to me, with blazing eyes: "We all

one bigga da Union. I.W.W.—dat word is pierced de heart of de
people!" (30)

Reed's description of these men penetrates beyond surface stereotypes. He does
romanticize them, but he comes closer than Williams in describing the meaning of
their suffering—after all he had a closer look during the strike. It should be noted,
however, that both writers manage to convey the major problem of hunger during
the strike, as well as the unity of the strikers.

Aside from the prejudicial quality of Williams' description, his
representation of the masses does indicate his comprehension of how their labor
shapes them. He offers the following description of the men and women's body
parts:

Below the skirt the ugly legs of the young girls

Pistons too powerful for delicacy!

The women's wrists, the men's arms, red,

Used to heat and cold, to toss quartered beeves

And barrels and milk cans and crates of fruit! (CP1 31)

His alarming reference to the young girls' legs as pistons illustrates the extent of
the dehumanization occurring in this industrial center. These girls have been
transformed into the machines that they operate. Lawson finds this description an
"abrupt switch." He claims, "Nature and culture reverse their polarities: it is the
machine which has an organic wholeness, the human is a monstrous hybrid of
flesh and mechanism" (11-12). The color red is also telling in this description. It
stood as the dominant I.W.W. color. In Wolff's poem "On Seeing the Garment
Strikers March," he describes a "Red Sea of Revolution" (12). In his tribute poem
to Elizabeth Gurley Flynn, Wolff describes her waving a blood-red banner with
the revolutionary motto: "Death to all masters! Freedom to all slaves!" (58). The
color red thus carries powerful connotations in a poem related to the 1913 silk
strike. In consideration of Williams' description of the women's wrists and the
men's arms, this color clearly indicates their working class status. It symbolizes

what Bill Haywood describes as the "red badge of toil." In particular, Haywood relates an incident when Elizabeth Gurley Flynn was speaking to the Paterson strikers about the meaning of the red flag. A striker interrupted her to show his flag: "And aloft he held his right hand—stained a permanent bloody crimson, gnarled from years of toil, and corroded by the scarlet dye which it was his business to put into the fabrics worn by the dainty lady of the capitalist class as well as by the fawning prostitute" (207). Such an incident dramatizes the powerful associations between red, the I.W.W., and the laboring men and women of Paterson. As Williams makes apparent in "The Wanderer," the strikers have been reduced to beasts and machines through their work. Through his perception of this dehumanization, the poet identifies the source of the divisions evident in this place—the capitalism and industrialization planted by Alexander Hamilton.

The poet's observation of the Paterson strike transforms him. The strikers' solidarity and brutality reduce him from the earlier Adamic poet to a shrieking infant:

> Ugly, venomous, gigantic!
> Tossing me as a great father his helpless
> Infant till it shriek with ecstasy
> And its eyes roll and its tongue hangs out—!
>
> I am at peace again, old queen, I listen clearer now. (CP1 31)

By reducing him to the feeling of a helpless infant, the 1913 strike has brought this poet into being. The silent strikers have exposed the serious divisions in American society and the poet has taken note. This knowledge has solidified his vocation. In Ernest Poole's *The Harbor*, the strikers have a similar type of effect on the narrator: "I found myself striving day and night to feel not one but thousands of men, a blurred bewildering multitude. And slowly in my striving I felt them fuse together into one great being, look at me with two great eyes, speak to me with one deep voice, pour into me with one tremendous burning passion for the freedom of mankind. Was this another god of mine?" (321). For both men the crowd becomes one, whether father or god, and calls them into a new level of being.

In "Caviar and Bread Again," Williams subscribes to the belief that the poet has the responsibility "when the race has gone astray, to lead it—to destruction perhaps, but in any case, to lead it" (SE 102). In the previous lines from "The Wanderer," the poet appears to come to the realization that he is needed, that he has a purpose in his modern world. Because of this understanding, he regains peace as the section concludes. He also makes a vow to "listen clearer" to the commands of his muse and to the language of the people who live in this place.

This section's turbulent sociohistorical context emerges in its very structure, especially in Williams' stanzaic structure and line-breaks. For example, the section includes seven stanzas, which far outnumbers the stanzaic breaks in the other sections. The section also has three line indentions; the other sections do not include any indentions. Also, Williams sets individual lines apart from a formal stanza. With these structural breaks, the section's form reflects the social breakdown occurring in Paterson. The momentary empowerment of these strikers has disrupted the traditional power structure and fostered the possibility for something new to emerge.

After perceiving the brutality of his modern world, the poet is taken from Paterson to a rural scene in the Jersey mountains in the next section, "Abroad." Observing the pastoral landscape of a country road and house, the muse orders him to speak to this rural world. He follows her command and yells out:

> Waken! O people, to the boughs green
> With unripe fruit within you!
> Waken to the myriad cinquefoil
> In the waving grass of your minds!
> Waken to the silent Phoebe nest

Under the eaves of your spirit! (CP1 32)

Without commenting upon his grand oratory, the muse draws the poet's attention to farmers in oat-fields with horses and "the weight of the sky" upon them. The poet tries again shouting loudly. Frail interprets the poet's call as "holding up the moral superiority of Jefferson's yeoman farmer—drawing his virtue from his intimacy with nature—to the factory dwellers and the boulevardiers" (90-91). However, it is important to point out that the poet's call is ineffective. His "voice was a seed in the wind" and his muse actually laughs at him (CP1 32). Despite all he has come into contact with through wandering in the modern world, the poet still speaks in an outdated voice. Lawson does not support Frail's "political" interpretation either. "Jeffersonian agrarianism, which is seen to be an anachronism," he argues, "can no longer serve as a source of transcendent individual freedom, just because it is a historical product, and a historically defeated one" (14). The muse's laughter mocks the poet's failure—he is still not the poet of modernity that he desires to be. After his failure to express this modernity, his muse abruptly "seizes" him and transports him back east towards the industrial area of Northern New Jersey. She returns him to a familiar setting by the Hackensack, a place he knew as a boy. Although the place has not changed, the poet has: It was "All so old, so familiar—so new now" (CP1 33).

The next section "Soothsay" occurs eight days later. The muse continually repeats to the young poet the line, "Behold yourself old!" (33). Intent on moving the poet beyond his youthful poetic desires, she has put him into contact with experiences that would connect him to his modern world. As he attempts to respond to her, she interrupts him and "wistfully" tells him:

> Good is my over lip and evil
>
> My under lip to you henceforth,
>
> For I have taken your soul between my two hands
>
> And this shall be as it is spoken. (33-34)

She asserts her total control over his soul as a poet. She imparts knowledge of good and evil to him by bestowing a kiss. This kiss suggests another step in his initiation as a modern poet.

The final section of "The Wanderer," "St. James' Grove," occurs in Williams' hometown of Rutherford. In this section, the poet, who was reduced to an infant in the "Paterson" section, is ceremoniously baptized as a modern poet. The poet sets off with the muse past the houses of his friends, as though on any ordinary "errand." This journey, however, is far from ordinary.

The muse and the poet head down the hill by Santiago Grove to the Passaic river, "that filthy river" (CP1 34). As Lawson remarks, the river reflects the times: it "is half-water and half-sewage, half life and half death, an emblem of modernity as division. The river maintains the 'purity' of natural origins, as well as the degradation of modernity" (15). After the poet's extended wandering through city and countryside, his muse has brought him to a local place that he has been close to all his life. Because of its familiarity and filth, however, the poet has overlooked its poetic power. Now, though, the muse ties their existence together in a ceremonial rite:

> Raising the black water, then in the cupped palm
>
> She bathed our brows wailing and laughing:
>
> River we are old, you and I,
>
> We are old and in our state, beggars.
>
> Lo the filth in our hair! our bodies stink!
>
> Old friend, here I have brought you
>
> The young soul you have long asked of me. (CP1 34)

Both the mythic beauty and modern degradation of the Passaic river become an integral part of this poet: "Enter youth into this bulk! / Enter river into this young man!" (35). With the completion of his baptism, the poet feels an immediate difference:

> Then the river began to enter my heart
>
> Eddying back cool and limpid

> Clear to the beginning of days!
>
> But with the rebound it leaped again forward—
>
> Muddy then black and shrunken
>
> Till I felt the utter depth of its filthiness,
>
> The vile breath of its degradation,
>
> And sank down knowing this was me now. (CP1 35)

With his immersion into the river, the poet gains a new, modern identity based in his locale and loses a part of himself. He actually sees himself "Being borne off under the water." As Rod Townley contends, "the baptism / drowning in 'The Wanderer' welds the poet's consciousness to the actual world" (36). The poem concludes with the muse's tribute to the bond that has been forged between muse, river, and poet: "Live river, live in luxuriance / Rememb'ring this our son" (CP1 36). There is also a promise of "new wandering." Joseph Riddel suggests, "The 'new wandering' of the young poet is (to be) the on-going speech of the place, which is 'mostly silent'" (62).

Unlike his earlier imitative long poem, Williams did not burn "The Wanderer." The poem represents his journey from imitative poetry to a poetry grounded in his modern locale. Considering the importance of "Paterson—The Strike" in this transformation, Williams' passage through Paterson and the brutality of the 1913 silk strike should not be merely a footnote. This event, as it had on June 7, 1913 in Madison Square Garden, took center stage in Williams' most significant early poem. It indicates Williams' shift towards an expression of his locale. He observed the strike, whether in person or via newspapers and magazines, and saw an electrifying subject for poetry. Like Reed's pageant, he saw the power of presenting the actual and also saw the potential of this strike to signify the larger divisions prevalent in modern America. Williams' willingness to write about these divisions in "The Wanderer" marks a major turning point in his development as a modern American poet. Williams, however, was not through with the "dusty fight" of 1913 or the city of Paterson. As he admits in the poem, "It sank deep into the blood" (CP1 31). He accepted the challenge to "listen clearer" to the speech of this place and discover its "redeeming language." It would take some time and more wandering to work out his epic project, but this early journey taught him that this place and its "filthy" river always would be a part of his poetry—"it became me."

CHAPTER 3

WILLIAMS' CONTACT WITH AMERICA (1914-1925)

In "The Wanderer" William Carlos Williams asks the question, "How shall I be a mirror to this modernity?" (CP1 28). Like the 1913 Armory Show and the Paterson Pageant, Williams' answer to this question involved experimentation and contact with his modern locale. As a physician in Rutherford, Williams' own form of contact with his locale came through his treatment of the working-class people in his surrounding region. His house calls were, as he recalls, "a great ticket of admission to a lot of things" (A 296). These visits gave him a chance to listen and to observe people in their own element. Such intimate contact provided him with poetic materials. He explains:

> The poem springs from the half-spoken words of such patients as the physician sees from day to day. He observes it in the peculiar, actual conformations in which its life is hid. Humbly he presents himself before it and by long practice he strives as best he can to interpret the manner of its speech. (A 362)

Williams, the well-educated middle-class doctor, listened to the "half-spoken words" of his patients and worked to recreate them in his art. It was through this contact that he gained a broader understanding of what it meant to be an American and what it required to be a modern American artist.

The Struggle of the "Democratic Aristocrat"

Al Que Quiere! (1917) is Williams' first book of poetry following *The Tempers*. It contains many of the poems he published following 1913, including "The Wanderer." The title itself troubled Williams. His worry reveals his concern regarding the political dimensions of his art. In a letter to Marianne Moore, he remarked that the title *Al Que Quiere!*, which he translated as "To him who wants it" (SL 40), did not represent his book's true content. He feared that it was not "democratic." So, he added the following phrase: "The Pleasures of Democracy." Commenting upon his dilemma to Moore, Williams wrote:

> You see, I am a mixture of two bloods, neither of them particularly pure. Yet there is always in me a harking back to some sort of an aristocracy—probably of the gallows, or worse—that will have a hand in all my democratic impulses. Then again there is a certain broad-fingered strain in me that will always be handling an axe for budding King Charles Firsts. So I torture myself through life. (SL 40)

Although he asks Moore's advice, he decided a few days later to remove the second-part of the title. He changed it to *A Book of Poems/ Al Que Quiere!*—"a book of poems to him who wants it. Get me?" (Mariani 145).

Williams' aristocratic/ democratic ambivalence came across to others. Catherine Stecchini, a Secondary School English teacher who lived in Princeton, New Jersey, met Williams in West Haven, Connecticut in 1951. Williams wrote to Kathleen Hoagland that he had "noticed a fairly young woman rather attractive in appearance and with a definitely cultivated speaking voice" (SL 306). Mrs. Stecchini was on vacation with her husband Livio, a Classics professor at the University of Chicago who wrote his doctoral dissertation at Harvard on the history of money in Greece. Williams was amazed that he should "blindly run smack into a classic scholar at the shore in Connecticut" (307); Williams spent quite a lot of time alone with him. Mrs. Stecchini found Williams to be a humorous man who was especially kind to her two sons. Yet she also picked up on his ambivalence: "He had a certain aristocratic attitude and a certain democratic attitude, and he may have conceived of himself as a sort of democratic aristocrat." Mrs. Stecchini attributes this perception to her own sensitivities regarding labels used to describe her—"school teacher" and "Irish Catholic" (SL 306). Nevertheless, her perception of Williams' ambivalence corresponds with his own comment in the letter to Marianne Moore about the nature of his "two bloods." The tension of these "two bloods" continued to appear throughout his life and art.

Williams' decision to pull the split title of *Al Que Quiere!* suggests his anxiety over the book's political dimensions. He did not want to present himself as a political poet. In writing to Ed Brown in May 1917, he makes it clear, as Mariani suggests, that he was "no ideologue trying to create a closer bond of brotherhood through poetry" (790). He exclaims in the letter, "Shit! I hate brotherhood." Instead, what he was after was the spoken word—he was "word crazy." He admits,

> The rhythms of everyday speech drive me mad. [. . .] Ignorant people use the most idiotic words sometimes with a dignity, a force a depth of feeling that makes them glow and flare. [. . .] I try to imitate. I almost always fail. It is a pretty game. (qtd. Mariani 790-791)

Despite his strong talk to the contrary, Williams needed to develop some sort of bond with his "brother" in order to make contact with this "everyday speech." For him, this bond with lower-class individuals took the form of the doctor/ patient relationship.

The poems in *Al Que Quiere!* portray Williams' struggle to embrace his American locale. "[I]t showed," as Mariani suggests, "a clear and distinctively poetic American voice dealing with a variety of subjects in a characteristic mode" (145). "Sub Terra," the first poem of the collection, announces Williams' determination to write about his immediate surroundings. Williams refers to the poem as "Spring, the earth giving birth to a new crop of poets, showing that I thought I would some day take my place among them, telling them that I was coming pretty soon" (IWWP 21). Although he boldly attempts to assert himself, Williams still remains distant from these others. This is evident in his choice of a Latin title, which reflects in part his aristocratic "blood." He guesses he was "pretentious" by using it and admits that he was trying to appear as "a Latin scholar" (IWWP 21). The poem opens with the poet alone and in search of "fellows" to make up his band:

> Where shall I find you,
>
> you my grotesque fellows
>
> that I seek everywhere
>
> to make up my band? (CP1 63)

His "earthy" aesthetic has failed to provide him with the communal contact that he desires. Williams understands he is in a transitional stage as a poet. He has yet to realize "grotesque fellows" through his poetry: "though I see you clear enough / you are not there!" Barry Ahearn sees "Sub Terra" as pointing in two different directions: "backward to the aesthetic of the 1909 *Poems* and forward to the rest of the poems in *Al Que Quiere!* and beyond" (*Alterity* 57).

In describing his aesthetic, Williams promises nothing pretty or comforting:

> You to come with me
>
> poking into negro houses
>
> with their gloom and smell!
>
> in among children
>
> leaping around a dead dog!
>
> Mimicking
>
> onto the lawns of the rich!
>
> You!

> to go with me a-tip-toe,
>
> head down under heaven,
>
> nostrils lipping the wind! (CP1 64)

Williams intends to probe the depths of his local surroundings—he wants to "fathom / the guts of shadows!" (64). Dragging his readers beyond the conventional and antiseptic, Williams wants to expose them to forbidden places (like the negro houses) and startling images (of children playing around a dead dog). Those who join his grotesque band will read such poetry and more. His concluding commands, "head down" and "nostrils lipping the wind," evoke images of the young poet entering Paterson "hot for savagery" and determined to suck up the turbulent atmosphere of the strike. Similar to that experience, he crudely associates these primal expressions with the atmosphere of this "other" world.

Williams represents working-class figures throughout his collection, including people he knew through commercial transactions. For instance, he writes about the woman who delivered his eggs in "Woman Walking." She presents, according to Williams, "a quite different figure from the lovely milkmaids of the pastorals, not at all the Marie Antoinette kind of thing" (IWWP 22). He considers it a "blessing" to see her again and writes admiringly of her

> coming with swinging haunches,
>
> breasts straight forward,
>
> supple shoulders, full arms
>
> and strong, soft hands (I've felt them)
>
> carrying the heavy basket. (CP1 66)

Williams romanticizes her strong physical presence. He has touched her, and as a result has been touched by her. Such physical contact, which Williams finds so important, endears her to him. He wistfully longs to see her more often—"for a different reason / than the fresh eggs." Williams' desire to know her more fully suggests his desire to make her into something more than a working-class woman who delivers his eggs. According to Barry Ahearn, the poem exhibits the tension "between Williams's willingness to let the woman be herself (whatever that might be) and his need for someone who, like Poe's Helen, can serve as a personal icon" ("Poet" 24).

"K.McB" also reveals a tension in Williams' depiction of the working class. Mariani identifies "K.McB" as Kathleen McBride (146), a young woman from the state orphanage who Williams hired to help care for his boys (CP1 489). This arrangement carries obvious class implications, which is evident throughout the poem. The poem has a humorous tone; however, the speaker patronizingly addresses Kathleen as an "exquisite chunk of mud" (CP1 106). Such a line, as Ahearn suggests, "relegates her to the status of the common and the low—literally so" ("Poet" 26).

Williams attempts to move beyond this demeaning class representation. He urges her to

> Curl up round their shoes
>
> when they try to step on you,
>
> spoil the polish! (CP1 107)

The "they" Williams mentions, those with polished shoes, refers to the upper class who "step-all-over" the lower class. What Williams advocates here is remarkable—he tells her not to accept such mistreatment, and instructs her to oppose it. As Ahearn once again perceptively contends,

> Williams urges her to violate the usual relations between "social class" servants and their betters. [. . .] Kathleen should remind them [the upper-class] that the distinctions between classes are not permanently established, but erasable. (27)

He believes that Kathleen should transgress class barriers to enlighten others. Williams' commands to her, however, indicate that he cannot allow Kathleen to be herself. He instructs her on what to do:

> teach them a dignity

> that is dignity, the dignity
>
> of mud! (CP1 107)

This repetition and play on the word "dignity" and mud further reveals Williams' light-hearted patronizing attitude towards this young servant. He continues to try and mold her muddy form. Despite his radical sounding message about transgressing social divisions, Williams dominates Kathleen and thus subverts his democratic intent in portraying her.

Williams' "Pastoral" poems also reflect his struggle to represent the lower class. These poems, according to John Lowney, "explore the gap between pastoral ideals and modern American socioeconomic reality" (57). Williams, however, does not only explore these gaps, but attempts to overcome them with his own constructed meaning. In "Pastoral" ("The little sparrows"), he compares the walking of "the old man who goes about / gathering dog-lime" with that of "the Episcopal minister / approaching the pulpit" (CP1 71). He claims that the old laborer's tread is "more majestic" than the minister's. His comparative judgment again attempts to shape the subject's value and significance, as he attaches *his* meaning to the man.

Williams' other "Pastoral" ("When I was younger") describes his poetic transformation. No longer a young poet obsessed with poetic fame, he looks to make contact with the slums of the lower class. He admires the

> roof out of line with sides
>
> the yards cluttered
>
> with old chicken wire, ashes,
>
> furniture gone wrong;
>
> the fences and outhouses
>
> built of barrel-staves
>
> and parts of boxes, all,
>
> if I am fortunate,
>
> smeared a bluish green . . . (CP1 64)

Williams' perception of these "back streets" provides him with a unique aesthetic pleasure. He uses short unrhymed lines and colloquial phrases like "furniture gone wrong" to portray the distinct character of this place. As Williams admits, "Unconsciously I was playing with the form of the line, and getting into the American idiom" (CP1 481). He concludes his poem with the line: "No one / will believe this / of vast import to the nation" (65). Breslin sees such a comment as sermonizing; it creates an effect that "the poetry seems imposed on rather than discovered in the objects described" (53). Williams' closing comment is heavy-handed. It further demonstrates his need to construct the cultural significance of the subject. He continues to preach to his reader about what he deems as the importance of America's "back streets."

The most overt political poem in the collection is "Libertad! Igualidad! Fraternidad!" The poem moves from dehumanizing a workingman to a consolation and commiseration with him. The speaker first yells at a man who has pushed him aside.

> You sullen pig of a man
>
> you force me into the mud
>
> with your stinking ash-cart! (CP1 77)

His outburst degrades the man and reveals his prejudice. However, he quickly modifies his condescending attitude.

> Brother!
>
> —If we were rich
>
> we'd stick our chests out
>
> and hold our heads high!

The reference to the man as "Brother" enables the poet to identify with him. "Perhaps Williams recognizes his own sullenness," as David Frail contends, "for he turns the confrontation into an assertion of solidarity, erasing whatever differences exist because of unequal economic or social status" (106). Considering their shared sullenness, these two men appear to have been "destroyed" by the "dreams" associated with the poem's title—"Libertad! Igualidad! Fraternidad!" Although this is not an American phrase, it seems that these two men expected to realize these ideals in their social setting. Instead they have encountered the brutal reality of America.

Time has changed the meaning of the words in the title. The poet expresses such change:

> There is no more pride
>
> in horses or in reign holding.
>
> We sit hunched together brooding
>
> our fate. (CP1 77)

The poet and the ash-cart man hunched over and disconsolate conveys a powerful image of Williams' sympathy for the working class. It reflects the brotherhood Williams protested against in his letter to Brown. All that remains for the poet and the workingman is commiseration. The poem thus expresses Williams' ambivalence to the dreams associated with American democracy.

In "Portrait of a Woman in Bed," Williams takes great strides in representing his lower-class subject as she exists, and not as he would like her to appear. He does so by recreating the voice of Robitza, a poor Polish woman in need of medical attention. According to Thomas Whitaker, the poem presents "a forceful experiment in the pace and tone of a laconic American speech much more limited in diction and syntax than the poet's own" (44). Robitza speaks in a casual, direct tone from her bed to a landlord looking to evict her.

> Lift the covers
>
> if you want me
>
> and you'll see
>
> the rest of my clothes— (CP1 87)

With her clothes "drying in the corner," Robitza presents herself to the man in a practical, provocative manner.

She also defies a conventional American attitude. Contrary to the traditional American notions of hard work and "penny" saving, she declares,

> I won't work
>
> and I've got no cash.
>
> What are you going to do
>
> about it? (CP1 87)

Not only does she refuse to work hard and make money, she challenges the landlord's notion about it. She then claims possession of the house she lives in simply because, as she states, "I need it" (88). Her attitude directly opposes the American work ethic. "Her most distinctive feature," as Ahearn suggests, "is her refusal to show any respect for the ambitions and values commonly associated with those who pursue the American Dream" ("Poet" 25). She is streetwise, which the landlord seems unable to comprehend. When asked by him about the welfare of her boys, she responds,

> My two boys?
>
> —they're keen!
>
> Let the rich lady
>
> care for them—
>
> they'll beat the school
>
> or
>
> let them go to the gutter—
>
> that ends the trouble. (CP1 88)

Robitza's response reveals a mother who sees limited possibilities for her sons in American society. She refuses to provide for them; instead, she places the responsibility onto others. One way or another, they will all be provided for. She understands the way American society works: "I won't starve / while there's the Bible / to make them feed me." Meanwhile, Robitza refuses to accept assistance. She calls the county physician, presumably someone like Williams, a "damned fool" and she tells the landlord to "go to hell!" This virulent reaction seems to stem from the way these men have treated her. The landlord has evidently forgotten to close the door when he entered.

> You could have closed the door
>
> when you came in;
>
> do it when you go out.
>
> I'm tired. (88)

Robitza's confrontational tone and outright anger reveal her belief that this man has treated her poorly. Her dismissal of him and command to close the door thus enable her to assert control over him. In fact, since her voice is the only one present in the poem, she has in a way dominated him. In this poem, Ahearn contends, "Williams presents a woman of the social class without resort to cliché or stereotyped form" ("Poet" 25). Although this point is debatable, such a depiction signals Williams' capacity to move beyond his earlier constructions of the lower class as he searches to recreate the American idiom in his verse.

The final poem of *Al Que Quiere!*, "The Wanderer," anchors the entire collection. Mariani contends that its placement at the end of the book suggests that Williams thought of the poem "as an appendix, as a verification of his crossing into the fallen world for his songs" (147). He did make some changes to the poem for its inclusion in *Al Que Quiere!*. For instance, in the "Broadway" section, he tones down his muse's appearance as a prostitute; instead, even though "[h]er might [is] strapped in by a corset," he describes her as a "horrible old woman" with "lewd Jew's eyes" (CP1 110). Williams' use of this anti-Semitic trope illustrates that he has still not moved beyond ethnic and racial stereotypes. His disturbing use of this stereotype capitalizes on the economic dimensions of the "Broadway" section. Another significant alteration to the original version is that "Paterson—The Strike" is retitled "The Strike." This change seems to distance the poem from the controversial 1913 strike. Williams, however, does maintain his reference to the city in the text: "'Go!' she said, and I hurried shivering / Out into the deserted streets of Paterson" (CP1 111). The Paterson reference, therefore, keeps this section connected to its 1913 origins. Williams' work on this poem and on this section in particular indicates that he was continuing to work out his response to the strike and to the city.

Al Que Quiere! highlights a fundamental change in Williams' approach to creating poetry. As Rod Townley suggests, "One's reaction to the poems in *Al Que Quiere!* is likely to be the same as Williams' reaction to the Armory Show of 1913: a laugh of relief" (91). This relief is due to Williams' development. He has moved away from a poetry of abstractions to a poetry that represents his locale and its inhabitants. In this book of poems, Williams also attempts to overcome the feeling that he has "failed" the people of his locale, a feeling he first expressed when observing the strikers in "The Wanderer." Many of these poems reflect Williams' search to discover the best way for the poet to treat the lower class in poetry—to instruct and guide them or to represent the actual conditions of their lives. Williams' democratic and aristocratic impulses clash in *Al Que Quiere!* and thus reveal the intensity of his struggle to respond to the problems of American society in his poetry.

Williams' Contributions to the *Masses*

Williams did not include "Sick African" or "Chinese Nightingale" in *Al Que Quiere!*, but they appeared in *The Masses* in January 1917. In his essay "America, Whitman, and the Art of Poetry," Williams remarked that

> *Masses* cares little for poetry unless it has some beer stenches upon
> it—but it must not be beer stench. [. . .] [I]t must be an odor of
> hops and malt and alcohol blended to please whom it meant to
> please. Oh hell! (35)

He viewed the poetry printed in *The Masses* as the expression of "realistic" subjects in outdated forms. His publication in this magazine, which had a radical reputation in politics and a conservative reputation in the arts, therefore proves all the more extraordinary. Whether or not Williams subscribed to the radical politics that *The Masses* espoused, his appearance in the magazine suggests that he believed there was a place for his poetry in politics or vice versa. Although he never constructed definitive boundaries for such a relationship, his publication in *The Masses* reflects a willingness to have his poetry enter the political arena. Vainis Aleksa claims that Williams "wanted to explore the more political and culturally abrasive context of the *Masses*, which he saw as the legacy of the political nature of the bursts of modernism in 1913" (22). Even David Frail admits that this was "one of his few political gestures with his poetry [. . .]" (104). By appearing in the pages of a radical magazine like *The Masses*, these two poems assume a political dimension.

In the early years of *The Masses* there was, as William O'Neil remarks, an "acceptance of the universal tendency to see the Negro as an object of humor" (232). In a 1915 response to a criticism of *The Masses* depiction of African-Americans, Max Eastman writes, "because the colored people are an oppressed minority, a special care ought to be taken not to publish *anything* which their race-sensitiveness, or the race arrogance of the whites, would misinterpret" (233). It is evident that the magazine fell short of achieving this racial sensitivity with the publication of poems like "Tilly's Apology" (1916) and "Lee Crystal" (1917).

Williams' "Sick African" also relies on racial stereotypes to convey his perception of an African-American family. Here is the poem:

> Wm. Yates, colored,
>
> Lies in bed reading
>
> The Bible—
>
> And recovering from
>
> A dose of epididymitis
>
> Contracted while Grace
>
> Was pregnant with
>
> The twelve day old
>
> Baby:
>
> There sits Grace, laughing,

Too weak to stand. (CP1 59)

Ahearn interprets Yates's "highly suggestive" contraction of epididymitis to "the black man as sexual threat" and his Bible reading in terms of the piety of "Uncle Tom" ("Poetry" 19). Ahearn also sees Grace's laughing as suggestive of another stereotype—"they always find some humor in their plight" (19). Yes, Grace does laugh. In the context of the scene, however, it does not seem like a stereotypical attempt to find humor in a bad situation. Instead, it comes across as an embarrassed, uncomfortable laughter. Grace's situation is one that no person would want to face—physically weak, she must care for a new baby and an incapacitated and *perhaps* unfaithful spouse. How is this family going to survive? Williams does not tell us.

Williams' diagnostic account of this family carries with it distinct power relations. His three patients, Wm., Grace, and the baby, are incapacitated and vulnerable. As the attending physician, he has a privileged position over this poor, sickly family. Despite his use of racial stereotypes, he refrains from preaching to the family or his readers. His opening abbreviation, short descriptive lines, and matter-of-fact tone read like a medical observation. He provides the radical readers of *The Masses* a poem that uses an experimental form to portray a troubling social scene. In his poem about this vulnerable African-American family, Williams was in effect showing *The Masses* what they were artistically missing.

The other experimental poem that Williams published in *The Masses* is "Chinese Nightingale."

Long before dawn your light

Shone in the window, Sam Wu;

You were at your trade. (CP1 59)

This short imagistic poem contradicts any expectation of a traditional nightingale poem. Instead, Williams represents the long hours of the working class, as embodied by Sam Wu. Ahearn again sees the poem in regard to its stereotypical images. In his estimation, Williams "has still not escaped defining them [alien people] in quite pedestrian cultural terms" ("Poetry" 20). His plain poem is pure observation, but the image of the working man stands out like the light from the dark. The poet addresses Sam Wu, but he tells Sam nothing that he doesn't already know—the working-class must put in long hours to survive in America. Williams' publication of both poems suggests, as Aleksa remarks, that he wanted "to demonstrate that free-verse had the flexibility, despite its experimental form, to engage issues congenial to the socialist principles of the *Masses*" (22).

An Artistic Breakthrough

One of Williams' most innovative literary achievements is *Kora in Hell: Improvisations* (1920). This project began in response to the United States' entrance into World War I. Williams described the pre-war period as a springtime for American art. He writes,

> all that delight [. . .] was being blotted out by war. The stupidity, the calculated viciousness of a money-grubbing society such as I knew and violently wrote against; everything I wanted to see live and thrive was being deliberately murdered in the name of church and state. (A 158)

America's capitalistic drive to make money frustrated Williams. He saw no such drive to create art. It left him wondering—was there a place in this culture for the artist? John Reed also voiced such an opinion in an April 1917 article for *The Masses* entitled "Whose War?": "War means an ugly mob-madness, crucifying the truth-tellers, choking the artists, side-tracking reforms, revolutions, and the working of social forces" (164).

For Williams, *Kora in Hell* represents a significant turn away from conventional writing. A real energy pervades the writing and engages the reader's imagination. Besides the chapter headings and the lines separating improvisations from their commentaries, Williams does not impose a linear structure on *Kora in*

Hell. The improvisations simply reveal the fluctuations of a mind stimulated by its daily contact with people and places. In chapter XV Part 3, Williams offers an explanation of this process:

> *That which is heard from the lips of those to whom we are talking*
> *in our day's-affairs mingles with what we see in the streets and*
> *everywhere about us as it mingles also with our imaginations. By*
> *this chemistry is fabricated a language of the day which shifts and*
> *reveals its meaning as clouds shift and turn in the sky and*
> *sometimes send down rain or snow or hail.* (I 59)

Williams offers a glimpse into how his mind works. He claims that by discarding the "distinctions of rhyme and meter" modern poets, like himself, are able to "set down" the fluctuation of language. By discarding traditional poetic structures, "the imagination of the listener and of the poet are left free to mingle in the dance." Contrary to several of the poems from *Al Que Quiere!*, the modern poet refrains from imposing his order upon his subject. He does not construct a fixed response for the reader—"He is 'free,' just as is the poet . . ." (Wagner 22). Such freedom, as Breslin remarks, "presents readers with a set of radical challenges," which include "many gaps for us to fill in" (58). This type of free-play liberates the reader and thus frees him or her to create meaning.

Williams portrays diverse sights and sounds in *Kora in Hell*. He includes a variety of voices. Margueritte S. Murphy believes that "his interest in American idioms [. . .] appears in the Improvisations as a rich interplay of speech genres, so that here we see the prose poem exploit more fully Bakhtinian heteroglossia [. . .]" (98). The following improvisation offers a recreation of the interplay of multiple voices:

> Hark! There's laughter! These fight and draw nearer, we—fight
> and draw apart. They know the things they say are true bothways,
> we miss the joke—try to—Oh, try to. Let it go at that. There
> again! Real laughter. At least we have each other in the ring of

that music. "He saved a little then had to go and die." But isn't it the same with all of us? Not at all. Some laugh and laugh, with little grey eyes looking out through the chinks—but not brown eyes rolled up in a full roar. One can't have everything.

Going along an illworn dirt road on the outskirts of a mill town one Sunday afternoon two lovers who have quarreled hear the loud cursing and shouts of drunken laborers and their women, followed by loud laughter and wish that their bodies were two fluids in the same vessel. Then they fall to twitting each other on the many ways of laughing. (I 80)

The laborers quarrelling and laughing parallels the quarrelling and "twitting" lovers. The lovers, like the poet, struggle to understand the laborers, but they don't quite make it. After hearing the laughter, they desire to be a part of the music created by the laborers' voices. Significantly, this vocal dance occurs while all these people are off from work and outside the constructs of town. Without these structural controls, a certain linguistic freedom appears possible—it enables one to hear "Real laughter." This interplay of voices, which occurs on a Sunday afternoon, foreshadows Dr. Paterson's encounters in *Paterson* Book II, "Sunday in the Park."

A variety of people appear in *Kora in Hell*. For example, Williams describes the body of Jacob Louslinger who was discovered in a local cemetery. According to the examining physician, "Looks to me as if he'd been bumming around the meadows for a couple of weeks" (I 31). Not only does a dead "bum" appear in the text, but there is a drive with a syphilitic friend, the little Polish Father of Kingsland, and a promiscuous, slow-witted girl. The diverse figures and voices create, as Murphy suggests, "[a] patently heteroglossic text [. . . which] resonates with a plurality of voices that represents a sort of textual 'democracy'" (112). At one point, Williams expresses the democratic lesson of his observations: "After some years of varied experience with the bodies of the rich and the poor a man finds little to distinguish between them, bulks them as one and bases his working judgements on other matters" (I 46).

Charles Doyle contends that writing *Kora in Hell* was a "liberating process" for Williams (34). Looking at *Spring and All* (1923), one of Williams' strongest achievements, one can see how Williams' descent in *Kora in Hell* liberated him. Describing his creation of *Kora in Hell* in *Spring and All*, Williams writes,

> I let the imagination have its own way to see if it could save itself. Something very definite came of it. I found myself alleviated but most important I began there and then to revalue experience, to understand what I was at— (CP1 203)

The daily creation of the multi-voiced improvisations resulted in Williams' development of a more democratic tone in his poetry. Murphy convincingly argues that through the process of writing *Kora in Hell* Williams managed to displace "the poet's voice from its dominant or monologic position in the poem" (132). To express these multiple voices, Williams looked to create more open forms, which led to his creation of *Spring and All*.

Williams affirms the power of the imagination in *Spring and All*. Early in the book he declares, "To refine, to clarify, to intensify that eternal moment in which we alone live there is but a single force—the imagination. This is its book" (CP1 178). Williams' first chapter, Chapter 19, then presents an imaginative destruction of the world "for sweetest love" (179). Such an apocalyptic tone was not uncommon for the period, especially in the wake of T. S. Eliot's *The Wasteland* (1922). However, Williams' apocalyptic destruction does not mean the end; instead, through the imagination the world will "be made anew" (179). The chapter ends with the following declaration:

> it is spring by the Stinking River where a magnolia tree, without leaves, before what was once a farmhouse, now a ramshackle home

> for millworkers, raises its straggling branches of ivorywhite
> flowers. (180)

Although it is not directly stated, the river seems to be the polluted Passaic. The transformation of the farmhouse into a ramshackle home for millworkers illustrates the major changes that have occurred here. The pastoral has been replaced by the industrial: still, like the flowers of the magnolia tree that continue to bloom, the imagination continues to exist and function in this locale.

Williams sees the re-creative power of the imagination as the goal of art. With Spring approaching, there is a loosening of the imagination from "THE TRADITIONALISTS OF PLAGIARISM," which refers to Samuel Butler's categorization of those "who can properly employ that which has been made use of before" (CP1 185). By breaking down this tradition, Williams, like spring itself, begins to define his own thoughts about art and the imagination. He desires

> an escape from crude symbolism, the annihilation of strained
> associations, complicated ritualistic forms designed to separate the
> work from "reality"—such as rhyme, meter as meter and not as the
> essential of the work, one of its words. (189)

The imaginative destruction of these formal devices releases a purer mode of artistic expression. "Just as the imagination destroys the authority of literary tradition" according to Allen Dunn, "so it subverts social hierarchy, discovering an affinity with the privations of the lower class" (56). Significantly, Williams associates "imaginative, values" with the lives of the lower class, a people "without the power of expression" (CP1 220). He even aligns the force of the imagination with the revolutionary power of this class: "To the social, energized class—ebullient now in Russia the particles adhere because of the force of the imagination energizing them" (CP1 220). Dunn remarks, "Williams makes the surprising claim that poverty is like the imagination since it eliminates superfluity and forces the attention to adhere to the moment at hand" (56-57).

The poems included in *Spring and All* complement and accentuate

Williams' discussion. These untitled poems are interspersed with prose, foreshadowing the technique used in *Paterson*. For instance, after declaring "THE WORLD IS NEW," he presents a poem later titled "Spring and All." The poem describes a rural wasteland of "muddy fields," "dried weeds," "patches of standing water," and "leafless vines." Despite the outer appearance of sterility, something below the surface emerges—"sluggish / dazed spring approaches" (CP1 183). This stark entrance stresses the process of the burgeoning imagination—a process discussed throughout the book's early chapters.

Williams includes a wide range of poems in *Spring and All*. There is "The Right of Way," which recreates the sensory movement of driving a car. There is also "Shoot it Jimmy!" with its jazz-like improvisation. There is the often anthologized "The Red Wheelbarrow." And, there is "Rapid Transit," which responds to his critics and makes use of diverse materials from his local scene. Although Williams is primarily concerned with experimentation in line and rhythm, there is a social element present in these poems as well. One poem that reflects these social concerns is "To Elsie." The poem presents an unromantic view of America's poor. "Williams escapes," as Ahearn contends, "the temptation to idealize the social class" ("Poet" 28). The poem opens, "The pure products of America / go crazy" (CP1 217). This opening, with its alliterative emphasis on America's pure products and setting off of "go crazy," highlights the stagnancy that Williams perceives in contemporary American culture. These products, whether from Kentucky or "the ribbed north end of / Jersey," are defective. As Ahearn suggests, "This portion of the 'social class,' in its want of admixture, mirrors the sterility and degeneration of European aristocracy" (28). Williams does not portray a vibrant and productive landscape. Instead the lakes and valleys are "isolate" and populated by "deaf-mutes" and "thieves" (CP1 217). The sexual contact here is unproductive; it is merely a cheap promiscuity between "devil-may-care men" and "young slatterns." Young girls are "tricked out" with the "gauds" given by lustful men. Such trickery, as Williams sees it, shows that the imaginations of these men "have no // peasant traditions to give them / character / but flutter and flaunt // sheer rags." Nevertheless, the girls succumb to these tricks "without emotion / save numbed terror"; they also remain unable to "express" these experiences.

> A girl can be "rescued" from such a "desolate" environment. She will be
>> sent out at fifteen to work in
>> some hard-pressed
>> house in the suburbs—

>> some doctor's family, some Elsie— (CP1 218)

Elsie's move to the suburbs enables Williams to experience a different form of contact with "some" person from a different social class. As James Clifford remarks, "a troubling outsider turns up *inside* bourgeois domestic space. She cannot be held at a distance" (6). This contact between the poor girl and the middle-class doctor reveals something to him—she expresses with "broken // brain the truth about us." He thus gains a unique vantage point from which to perceive the impaired articulation of "truth" that she personifies.

Despite the change in locale, Elsie remains susceptible to the manipulation and exploitation of others. Instead of being "tricked out" by "devil-may-care men," she addresses herself to "rich young men with fine eyes." Her weakened imagination leaves her desiring finery and wealth. "[S]he embodies," as Breslin contends, "the national desire for quick, easy wealth" (69). Her desire for such wealth, however, results in an incomplete expression of her locale, "as if the earth under our feet / were / an excrement of some sky" (CP1 218). Her inability to express "earthly" contact reduces us to "degraded prisoners" who "hunger until we eat filth."

Meanwhile, in an effort to transcend her troubling presence in the poem, the imagination strains "after deer / going by fields of goldenrod in // the stifling heat of September." Such an imaginative escape, however, fails to confront the crude, incomplete expression of "truth" that has disrupted the poem. Williams understands that

> It is only in isolate flecks that
>
> something
>
> is given off

To know Elsie, he must accept the indeterminate "something" that constitutes her life and that resists his attempts at control. "From fitting Elsie into her historical and geographical process," Robert Pinsky remarks, "the poem reverses, strains to fit itself . . . into the context of her life" (25). Williams concludes by attempting to express her actual modern circumstance.

> No one
>
> to witness
>
> and adjust, no one to drive the car (219)

Williams reflects the uncertain, uncontrollable essence of modernity through his driverless car metaphor. Without imaginative contact with the locale, modern American society seems headed towards a destructive end. Williams accepts this uncertain state and emphasizes its unfinished quality by not ending the line with a period; he thus leaves the poem open. As John Palattella suggests, "the possibility for adjustment remains open, but at this time that change is impossible to manage" (14).

America: Past as Present

The Great American Novel (1923), written during the fall of 1921, reflects Williams' struggle to come to terms with what it meant to be an American artist in the 1920s. Originally he developed this project as a satirical response to the popular pursuit of writing the "great American novel." He describes it as "a satire on the novel form in which a little (female) Ford car falls more or less in love with a Mack truck" (A 237). Although the book is satirical, it also comments upon the "shoddy" state of contemporary American culture.

Williams' first chapter, "The Fog," begins with his drive for artistic progress. He lives in a place where the ground is hollow and time actually moves backwards. He wonders how to begin his project and settles on words. As he explains, "One must begin with words if one is to write" (I 158). He attempts to make and break words and becomes frustrated. He declares, "There cannot be a novel. There can only be pyramids, pyramids of words, tombs" (160). Chapter II opens with a declaration of newness. This newness relates to the technology of the time: "I'm new, says the great dynamo. I am progress. I make a word. Listen! UMMMMMMMMMMMMM—" (162). Despite a wrong turn in the fog, he still longs to liberate words and make them his own. He thinks he makes a discovery: "Clean, clean he had taken each word and made it new for himself so that at last it was new, free from the world for himself [. . .]" (167). He boasts of his discovery to his wife. She responds, "What did you say, dear, I have been asleep?" His quest is far from over; the writing of the "great" American novel must continue.

The subsequent chapters continue to explore the writer's desire to liberate the word. Chapter III, however, also delves into cultural concerns. It attacks the European literary tradition. Williams repeatedly calls for American artists to destroy this tradition. In Chapter V, he exclaims, "Europe is nothing to us. Simply nothing. Their music is death to us. We are starving—not dying—not dying mind you—but lean bellied for words" (174). Echoing Ralph Waldo Emerson and Walt Whitman, Williams announces that American artists must turn away from Europe and make contact with America. He even chides his American predecessors: "We look at that imitative phase with its erudite Holmeses, Thoreaus, and Emersons. With one word we can damn it: England" (211). Through his vilification of European art and his damning of American writers, Williams boldly attempts to clear the way for his own style of American art.

Like his 19th century predecessors, Williams wants American artists to embrace their American identity. To achieve any sense of artistic freedom, one must accept this cultural fact. Williams does:

> I am a beginner. I am an American. A United Stateser. Yes it's
> ugly, there is no word to say it better. I do not believe in ugliness.
> I do not want to call myself a United Stateser but what in—but
> what else am I? (I 175)

Though not fond of the term United Stateser, Williams refuses to discard it and soberly accepts his status as an American artist. Because of the culture's crudeness, however, such acceptance is not easy. Williams' does not gloss over this concern. In Chapter V, he declares,

> America is a mass of pulp, a jelly, a sensitive plate ready to take
> whatever print you want to put on it—We have no art, no manners,
> no intellect—we have nothing. We water at the eyes at our own
> stupidity. We have only mass movement like a sea. But we are
> not a sea— (I 175)

Williams offers a less than inspiring vision of American art, yet it is only because he believes that American artists have failed to make their "print" on this formless mass. It is the artist's duty to create something from this mass that is truly original and truly American. But, the artist must understand the brutal nature of this jelly-like mass. As Williams memorably exclaims,

> I am saying that America will screw whom it will screw and when
> and how it will screw. And that it will refrain from screwing when
> it will and that no amount of infiltration tactics from "superior
> civilizations" can possibly make us anything but bastards. (I 210)

Williams understands the rough side of American life, which stems from a competitive, materialistic society. He candidly admits that this omnipotent American screw is part of the American experience.

As Williams, a United Stateser, quests for the "word," he delves into America's past. Chapter VII opens with Columbus's sailors yelling out "Nuevo Mundo!" and ends with Columbus trying to communicate with the natives. This attempt at communication between European and Indian, this initial contact, represents the origins of America—"It was indeed a new world" (185). In Chapter XII, Williams relates De Soto's burial in the Mississippi river. For Williams, this burial represented a dissolving of the old world into the new—another form of immediate contact.

In subsequent chapters, Williams mentions other people connected to the New World: Eric the Red, Brigham Young, Abraham Lincoln, George Washington, Davy Crockett, and Aaron Burr. Significantly, he juxtaposes Burr with an advertisement for Pisek fashions that appeals to "a fastidiously fashionable clientele" and matches designs to their "charms, characteristics and station" (I 190-191). Following this advertisement, Williams praises Aaron Burr's unlimited potential for greatness. These possibilities end, however, with his killing of Hamilton—"For you everything is possible. Bing! and Hamilton lies dead" (I 191). The juxtaposition of the high-society advertisement and Burr's lost possibilities creates a simultaneous experience of the past and present. Would this class-conscious advertisement appear if Burr, who Williams portrays as a true democrat, had not been vilified for killing the Federalist Hamilton? Such a reading may seem to be forced. But, Williams presents a fashion advertisement, Burr's lost possibilities, and the prostrate body of Hamilton. For Williams, the Burr-Hamilton duel decided the fortunes of both men and quite possibly the future of the country.

Williams also comments upon contemporary America's obsession with money. In Chapter XII, he illustrates this greed in a collection notice for one dollar. The notice questions the debtor's honesty and threatens to notify an extensive financial network: "The bank will take note of it. From there the information quietly passes to the various Mercantile Agencies, Dun's, Bradstreet's, Martindale's" (I 203). In Chapter XVII, Williams portrays the simple, almost primitive lives of people in the Southern mountain range of the Cumberland. For the most part, their lives "have changed so little that they are in many ways the typical Americans" (220). One of these "typical" Americans is Ma Duncan who is "straight and sure-footed as an Indian" who offers the following commentary regarding contemporary America: "I wish you could have seen the great old trees that used to be here. If folks wasn't so mad for money they might be here and a preachin' the gospel of beauty. But folks is all for money and all for self" (219). Ma Duncan's comment exposes the gap between a modern materialistic America and an idealistic America. In the subsequent chapter, Williams contrasts Ma Duncan's idealism with some classic American rags-to-riches stories. He mentions, for example, men like C.C.A. Baldi who made a "great business" out of lemons (221). "This section of the composition," according to Norma Procopiow, "pertains to Williams' interest in the idealistic versus materialistic concerns in American life. Clearly his view is that the latter has gained dominance" (165).

The novel concludes with a description of the production of shoddy, a cheap cloth processed from woolen rags. Shoddy embodies the state of American culture. Williams remarks, "You've seen this fake oilcloth they are advertising now. Congoleum. Nothing but building paper with a coating of enamel. *O Vida tan dulce!*" (I 227). These lines underscore Williams' perception of America's shallowness—its devotion to sweetness and not to substance.

The Great American Novel expresses Williams' determination to discard fixed forms and to utilize the materials available to him as an American artist. Mariani writes that he takes these materials "and mix[es] them all into the hopper, grease and all, to create a viable mirror of the times: the American novel as shoddy" (190-191). He does not create a flattering portrait of American culture. He portrays an America that is artistically crude, stupid, and shallow; it is a culture driven to make money, not art. Nevertheless, as the existence of this novel shows, Williams refuses to turn away.

Williams makes further contact with American materials in *In the American Grain* (1925). Williams does not regurgitate facts in this collection of essays, but rather refashions and refreshes a conceptual understanding of

American history. Paul L. Jay describes Williams' "historiographic art" as composed of two "inter-locking conceptions" (21). He claims that for Williams "history must remain 'undecided' and 'open,' and that it must be given unity and regenerative power by the artist." Williams writes essays on both traditional and non-traditional American figures. He devotes chapters to Christopher Columbus, George Washington, Benjamin Franklin, and Cotton Mather; however, he also includes chapters on Red Eric, Pere Sebastian Rasles, Thomas Morton, and Aaron Burr. As Brian Bremen contends, Williams' presentation of these diverse figures is an attempt "to expose what history *is* by revealing a Puritan tradition of domination and subversion at the textual level, and to suggest what history *should be* by including those voices that tradition has repressed or silenced" (142).

Stylistically, Williams approaches each chapter differently. As he explains,

> The Tenochtitlan chapter was written in big, square paragraphs like Inca masonry. Raleigh was written in what I conceived to be Elizabethan style; the Eric the Red chapter in the style of the Icelandic saga; Boone in the style of Daniel's autobiography
>
> [. . .] (A 183-184)

For some chapters, Williams paraphrases an original source or relies heavily on direct quotes; for other chapters, he creates first person narratives or dialogues. *In the American Grain* therefore brings together a unique collection of American voices.

Williams' presentation of these different voices reflects his emphasis upon making contact with America. Contact is a key word in Williams' study. To be truly American and truly heroic in Williams' eyes, one must make contact with the spirit of America. He illustrates this contact by men as different as De Soto, Pere Sebastian Rasles, and Daniel Boone. In "De Soto and the New World," he intersperses his narrative of De Soto's journey to the Mississippi with addresses from "SHE," the voice of the American wilderness. "SHE" speaks of her love and desire to become one with De Soto: "You will not dare to cease following me [. . .] turning from the sea, facing inland" (IAG 45). For Williams, De Soto's pose—facing inland—is distinctly American; it represents a turning away from Europe towards the New World. Another person who turned away from Europe and made contact with America was the Frenchman Pere Sebastian Rasles. For thirty-four years Rasles lived with a tribe of Native Americans, "drawing their sweet honey, TOUCHING them every day" (120). Williams also portrays Daniel Boone as a man unafraid to touch. Alone in the Kentucky wilderness he wanted "to bathe in, to explore always more deeply, to see, to feel, to touch [. . .] to understand it and to be part of its mysterious movements—like an Indian" (137). All three men express in their own ways a willingness to make contact with America.

The main oppositional force to this form of contact is the abstraction of Puritanism. Williams believes that Puritanism interfered with the realization of a truly New World, a place where individual contact with the locale would produce a race of truly liberated men and women. With their emphasis on the spirit over the flesh, Puritans failed to make productive contact with the continent. Attempts to make such contact, as evident in the Thomas Morton chapter, were seen as a threat to order and control. Williams expresses his anger toward Puritanism in a conversation with the Frenchman Valery Larbaud.

> There is a "puritanism"—of which you hear, of course, but you have never felt it stinking all about you—that has survived to us from the past. It is an atrocious thing, a kind of mermaid with a corpse for tail. Or it remains, a bad breath in the room. This THING, strange, inhuman, powerful, is like a relic of some died out tribe whose practices were revolting. (IAG 115)

Williams blames Puritanism for America's contemporary problems. For him, the Puritans' failure to make contact with their locale has led to social divisions, dehumanization, and a strict authoritarian government—"Everything is

Federalized and all laws become prohibitive in essence" (128). This may place too much blame upon the Puritans, but it reveals Williams' devotion to contact and his frustration with American society.

Williams is also frustrated with America's insatiable appetite for wealth. With such greed and materialism, there inevitably occurs inequality—not everyone can be rich. Williams recognizes this divisive reality:

> The poor are ostracized. Cults are built to abolish them, as if they were cockroaches, and not human beings [. . .] Let everybody be rich and SO EQUAL. What a farce! But what a tragedy! It rests upon false values and fear to discover them. Do not serve another for you might have to TOUCH him and he might be a JEW or a NIGGER. (176-177)

For Williams, the principle of equality in America is an illusion—how can there be equality in a capitalist system? Will the "other" really be treated equally in the eyes of the law? Instead of such equality, Williams perceives a society that abhors contact with "others" and discriminates against their differences.

Williams' chapter on Aaron Burr, "The Virtue of History," examines the historical origins of this inequality. He structures the chapter as a debate between two "voices"—one holding a traditional view of Burr and the other, a revised image of him. The remarks of the traditional voice incite the other voice to defend Burr's actions. This other voice refuses to trust historical interpretations of Burr's motives: "Burr's account in history is a distortion. The good which history should have preserved, it tortures" (197). He wants to loosen Burr from a prejudicial historical definition and examine him in his times "as a living thing, something moving, undecided, swaying [. . .]" (192). This distrustful attitude towards the objectivity of history underlies Williams' entire book. Although he constructs his own version of history, Williams recognizes, according to Paul Jay, that "history is a product of representation" and consequently he deconstructs the "innocent relationship between historical events and their existence in narrative"

(24).

For Williams, Burr personifies the "true element" of liberty (IAG 195). When the Revolutionary War concluded, the new nation faced a critical decision. Was it going to honor its pre-war promises of liberty and freedom? Or, was it going to slip back into yet another form of a controlling government? According to Williams, "The sense of the individual, the basis on which the war was fought [. . .] began to be debauched. [. . .] Burr sensed it" (194). Burr steadfastly believed that the war was fought to provide total liberty. As Williams later contends, "Burr knew what a democracy must liberate. [. . .] Men intact—with all their senses waking" (206). Burr's commitment to ensure this form of liberty, according to Williams, caused him to be labeled a "subversive force" (194).

Washington, Jefferson, and many others disliked Burr. But his greatest enemy was the Federalist Alexander Hamilton. Williams vilifies Hamilton throughout this chapter. He portrays Burr as the true, but forgotten, voice of liberty and Hamilton as the agent of tyranny. He refers to Hamilton as "a balloon of malice" and Washington's "shrewd dog" (190; 197). No doubt Williams' admiration for Burr originates in his killing of Hamilton. Bryce Conrad agrees: "Burr's privileged place in *In the American Grain* arises [. . .] because Burr happened to perform a great symbolic act in Williams' vision of American history: he shot Hamilton" (263).

Williams was no lover of the Federal Government or capitalism—two systems championed by Hamilton. Also, Williams despised Hamilton for his industrialization of Paterson. The city still retains Hamilton's imprint.

> Paterson he wished to make capital of the country because there
> was waterpower there which to his time and mind seemed colossal.
> And so he organized a company to hold the land thereabouts, with
> dams and sluices, the origin today of the vilest swillhole in
> christendom, the Passaic River; impossible to remove the nuisance
> so tight had he, Hamilton, sewed up his privileges unto

> kingdomcome, through his holding company, in the State legislature. *His* company. *His* United States: Hamiltonia—the land of the company. (IAG 195)

Obviously, for Williams, Hamilton's will dominates American society. Williams abhors such control. As Conrad explains, "Hamilton raped and pillaged the very place that would become the site of Williams' own attempts to marry the ground" (263). Williams could not forgive such an act and would continue to struggle with Hamilton until the very end of *Paterson*.

Considering these strong feelings about Hamilton's corruption of the Passaic Falls and Paterson, it is only natural that Williams treats Burr as a maltreated hero. He finds Burr's involvement in a plan to invade Mexico as a pursuit of liberty, not a traitorous act. He never even mentions Burr's solicitation of foreign assistance to conquer Florida. No, Williams portrays Burr as possessing "[a] humanity, his own, free and independent, unyielding to the herd, practical, direct" (IAG 204). This heroic portrayal of Burr lies in the fact that "[h]e killed his man, logically and as he meant to do and knew he must" (201). Williams drew inspiration from Burr's act, for he too had to oppose Hamilton.

"If Americans are to be blessed with important work," Williams wrote in a 1921 issue of *Contact*, "it will be through intelligent, informed contact with the locality which alone can infuse it with reality" (RI 68). As evident from his work between 1914-1925, Williams made contact with his locality on diverse levels. His work as a doctor brought him in touch with the working class of Northern New Jersey; his work as a poet not only brought him into imaginative contact with these patients, but also with the people who shaped the history of the place. These different forms of contact altered Williams' approach to creating poetry and prose. As Williams wrote in an earlier issue of *Contact*, "We believe that in the perfection of that contact is the beginning not only of the concept of art among us but the key to the technique also" (RI 66). While Williams worked out this artistic technique, he also continued to work out his thoughts about the city of

Paterson. Whether it was in the reworking of "The Wanderer" for *Al Que Quiere!*, the drunken laughter of mill workers in *Kora in Hell*, the ramshackle home for mill workers in *Spring and All*, or the references to the Burr—H amilton conflict in *The Great American Novel* and *In the American Grain*, the city of Paterson and the lives of its mill workers were not far from Williams' mind. His "intelligent" and "informed" contact with this American locale would prove to be the source of the "important work" he would produce in the upcoming years.

CHAPTER 4

"SOUNDING OUT" THE DEPTHS OF PATERSON

In a November 1936 letter to Ezra Pound, William Carlos Williams writes, "And then there's that magnum opus I've always wanted to do: the poem PATERSON. Jeez how I'd like to get at that. I've been sounding myself out in these years working toward a form of some sort [. . .] " (SL 163). Throughout the years leading up to his publication of *Paterson* Book I (1946), Williams continually sounded himself out about Paterson in his poetry and prose. This "sounding out" period coincided with his attempt to negotiate through the sociopolitical mine field of the 1930s. Williams repeatedly flirted with radical politics. He became affiliated with the proletarian publication *Blast*, participated in the Social Credit Movement, and contributed to both the *New Masses* and *Partisan Review*. Yet Williams refused to create art that served a particular ideology. He understood what John Reed expressed to Max Eastman: "this class struggle plays hell with your poetry!" ("Memoir" 77). Thus, as Williams continued to sound himself out about *Paterson*, he explored carefully the relationship between art and politics.

In 1926, *New Masses* asked Williams for a contribution; he sent them the short story "The Five Dollar Guy." Upon seeing his story in the magazine, Williams knew that he had a serious problem—he had forgotten to change the names of the people involved in the incident. He feared the consequences of the impending lawsuit. "If the case went to a jury," as Mariani explains, "Williams knew it would take just one rabid middle-class woman looking at the cover of *New Masses*—that Communist rag—to convict him" (254). Like his previous contribution to the *Masses*, Williams' contribution to the *New Masses* illustrates his desire to present his work in the pages of a radical political magazine. Yet, along with his desire to be heard in such a radical political forum, existed his fear of being defined, or, as the above scenario suggests, being convicted as a "political" poet. As discussed with *Al Que Quiere!*, this label was one that Williams wanted to avoid. In the end, Williams never faced a legal conviction for his story because he agreed to pay $5,000 and "promised" never to publish it again (255).

Where was Williams going to find an extra $5,000 to pay-off his legal settlement? Just as he faced this question, he received *The Dial's* 1926 award for poetry, which included a $2,000 cash prize. *The Dial* award money answered some of Williams' financial problem, but, more importantly, it recognized his poetry, specifically the poem "Paterson." This poem is a noteworthy step in the development of *Paterson*. It functioned, as Williams claims, as the basis for his "later and more extended poem" (A 243). At this time, according to Mariani, "eighty-five lines was about as long as he could coax his imagist muse into flying for him" (263). Nancy Barry, however, notes that earlier versions of the poem are much longer than the published version (218 lines and 249 lines); she even remarks, "their form seems quite close to the published version of Book One" ("Fading" 347). These lengthy early drafts indicate the scope of Williams' project. The eighty-five lines that he did publish, therefore, offer a valuable glimpse into his early thoughts about the city as poetic material.

The poem begins during a transitional time "when there is nothing" (CP1 263). A gap exists "in the pause between / snow and grass," which offers a chance for something new and different to emerge. The poet attempts to represent this changing scene and exclaims, "—Say it, no ideas but in things—." This declaration, which occurs twice more, asserts the primacy of actual "things." It announces his attempt to reunify words with the "things" they represent in order to overcome the fragmentation and division existent in this place. Following his interjection, Williams describes the nothingness that pervades the scene—"the blank faces of the houses / and cylindrical trees." These "things" lack wholeness and perfection. They are "split, furrowed, creased, mottled, stained / secret." They reflect the divisive features of this place. Yet they also embody Paterson's ideas:

> These are the ideas, savage and tender
>
> somewhat of the music, et cetera
>
> of Paterson, that great philosopher— (CP1 263)

Williams describes the city as a man, a concept inspired, in part, by his reading of James Joyce's *Ulysses* (IWWP 72). He claims, "The thing was to use the multiple facets which a city presented as representative for comparable facets of contemporary thoughts [. . .]" (Thirlwall 254). As evident by the multiple, contradictory nature of his ideas, Paterson emerges as a complicated modern figure/ place.

It also should be mentioned that the concept of a man/ city is similar to an image presented during the 1913 Paterson silk strike Pageant. The pamphlet cover, designed by Robert Edmond Jones (Wertheim 54), shows a larger-than-life mill worker emerging from the background of darkened factories with his right hand raised—literally a man/ city. Ben Shahn, whom Williams mentions in *Paterson* (183; 211), gave Williams the painting *Homage to Paterson*. Williams accepted the gift but commented to a friend, "I'd like to have seen a big figure of a mill-worker applied all over the surface of it with the windows showing through" (Mariani 608). It would be hazardous to make a direct correlation between the pamphlet and Williams' notion of the man/ city, but it does offer further insight into his visualization of this figure.

After he identifies the ideas of the great philosopher, Williams depicts the life source of Paterson—the Passaic River. The river descends "[f]rom above, higher than the spires, higher / even than the office towers [. . .]" (CP1 263). Williams emphasizes the fact that it appears higher than both the church and business community. The Falls possess a divine-like quality that "crashes" down upon the city "in a recoil of spray and rainbow mists—" (CP1 264). In this continual, explosive fall of water Williams once again interjects, "Say it, no ideas but in things—." Amid this constant flux, he attempts to represent the features of this place and writes of "factories crystallized." His contrast between the Falls' "rainbow mists" and "factories crystallized" indicates its industrial transformation. Its pure aesthetic value has been replaced by its industrial and economic value. This revaluation brings a momentary halt to the poem, which Williams indicates by using a series of ellipses.

The second part of "Paterson" begins with an intensified command, "Say it! No ideas but in things." This heightened intensity comes from the knowledge that "Mr. / Paterson has gone away / to rest and write." In spite of this departure, Paterson's "thoughts" remain—personified in the actual people living and working in the city. He perceives these thoughts in the city bus: "Inside the bus one sees / his thoughts sitting and standing" (CP1 264). He cannot comprehend these transitory people. Their movement leads him to ask:

> Who are these people (how complex
>
> this mathematic) among whom I see myself
>
> in the regularly ordered plateglass of
>
> his thoughts, glimmering before shoes and bicycles—? (CP1 264)

These people, like the strikers in "The Wanderer," seem impenetrable to him. Like the silent strikers, "They walk incommunicado." However, he does come away with some understanding: "the / equation is beyond solution, yet / its sense is clear." He realizes the impossibility of understanding the group in its entirety.

Williams turns from the crowd to one specific person—Alex Shorn, the boot-black's son. He describes the boot-black's house painted with images of mythological figures. These painted walls, which mask the actual interior of the place, do not bring him any closer to the people of Paterson. His tone becomes more insistent: "But who! who are these people?" (CP1 264). He understands that they comprise the "savage and tender" thoughts of Paterson. After all, "It is / his flesh making the traffic, cranking the car / buying the meat—." Yet he has failed to know the living nature of these people. Consequently, he stops trying to make meaning of their lives. Then, they

> fall back among cheap pictures, furniture
>
> filled silk, cardboard shoes, bad dentistry
>
> windows that will not open, poisonous gin
>
> scurvy, toothache— (CP1 264-65)

He perceives their fragmented nature through the crude "things" that compose their lives.

Williams continues to work toward an understanding of this modern man who is a city in the third part of "Paterson." He insists that Paterson's basic "thoughts are decorous and simple," but in this modern world there is "the despair and anxiety // the grace and detail of / a dynamo" (265). This dynamo reference echoes Henry Adams' despair amid the technological advances of his modern age. He develops this Adams-like despair more fully with the exclamation "Divine thought!," which evokes the Virgin and Dynamo dichotomy of Adams' *Education*. Williams then provides a literal example of how modern technology has broken man with the story of Jacob who "fell backwards off the press / and broke his spine." This machine-related accident renders Jacob's "perfect" legs "without movement or sensation." Interestingly, the connection between man and machine in "Paterson" echoes the description of the young women in "The Wanderer"; he compares their ugly legs to "[p]istons too powerful for delicacy!" (CP1 31). In that earlier poem, the women are transformed into machines. In "Paterson" Williams again associates the worker and machine, yet this time a worker is literally broken and paralyzed through his work with the machine. Returning to his earlier alignment of religion/ industry, Williams follows Jacob's accident with an account of postal clerks stealing rare stamps from the Pope's monthly letters to Mr. Paterson. These incidents of paralysis and theft illustrate both the force of this power structure and the subversion of it.

The fourth and final part of "Paterson" presents varied images. It continues with the children and stamps, but the noun "stamp" becomes a verb as the children are "stamping the snow." Then, there is "[t]he actual, florid detail of cheap carpet" (CP1 265). Williams juxtaposes this staid covering with a canary "singing" and the "spreading" leaves of geraniums "reflecting red upon the frost" (CP1 265). These basic, mundane particulars—these "things"—illustrate the changing nature of Paterson. As Williams writes,

> They are the divisions and imbalances
>
> of his whole concept, made small by pity
>
> and desire, they are—no ideas beside the facts—
>
> (CP1 265-266)

Williams creates imbalance in the lines and disrupts a fixed meaning of the objects that constitute Paterson. Ultimately, he achieves a sense of disruption by altering his refrain from "Say it, no ideas but in things" to "they are—no ideas beside the facts." According to F. Douglass Fiero, these lines imply "that this is still a beginning" (970).

Williams' poetic struggle in "Paterson" is similar to his experience as an observer of the Paterson strike in the poem "The Wanderer." In that early poem, Williams walks among the strikers on the bread-line and tries to communicate with them. They do not respond. At this stage in his writing, though sympathetic to the brutal struggle of these people, Williams cannot express the actual rhythm of their speech in his verse and relies on crude stereotypes to describe them. His inability to express their voices stems, in part, from his social difference—their lives and struggles remain apart from his personal experience. In "Paterson,"

Williams again tries to "know" the people, the thoughts of Paterson. Once again, though, he fails to gain this knowledge. He asks in part two of the poem, "But who, who are these people?" His question, however, remains unanswered. Yes, he has heard these people speak and he wants to express this speech in his poetry—their language is the key to the development of the poem. Still, he remains unable to express the fluctuating nature of their voices.

"Life Along the Passaic River" as Art, not Politics

In 1933, Williams returns to Paterson as a subject for his short story "Life Along the Passaic River." During the Great Depression, many artists, like Williams, felt the pressure to create art that served a political end. In his essay "The Basis of Faith in Art," Williams describes this pressure: "You gotta write propaganda today. You know, yuh gotta 'help humanity'—" (SE 182). Williams continually struggled with how far he would commit his art to politics. "By 1930, it was clear, aesthetics were rapidly giving way to social and political concerns," Mariani explains, "but Williams was too radical, really, to swing all the way in that direction" (300). "Life Along the Passaic River" is a short story that demonstrates Williams' approach to this artistic-political dilemma. He portrays the lower-class people living around the river, but he refrains from attaching an overt political commentary or moral message to his story. In "A Beginning on the Short Story," he writes:

> I lived among these people. [. . .] I saw how they were maligned
> by their institutions of church and state—and "betters." [. . .] I
> saw how stereotype falsified them. [. . .] It was my duty to raise
> the level of consciousness, not to say discussion, of them to a
> higher level, a higher plane. Really to tell. (SE 300)

This sense of "duty" epitomizes Williams' overall approach to representing the poor people of his locale.

In Twain-like fashion, "Life Along the Passaic River" opens with a small boy in a self-made canoe floating on the river in July. Yet this is not Twain's mighty Mississippi but the industrialized and polluted Passaic. The Manhattan Rubber Co. discharges water "from a pipe at the foundation level below the factory [. . .]" (CS 109). As Reed Whittemore contends, "Life along the Passaic River was rough in the thirties and WCW left no doubt of that; but he also left no doubt that life was being lived there" (251).

Besides the river, a common bond of economic hardship unites the inhabitants. A diverse group of people inhabits the region: Blacks, Italians, and Poles. For the most part, they appear idle and unemployed. Williams picks up one of these idlers on a corner. After an exchange of pleasantries and cigarettes, the conversation turns to work:

> Looking for work? Just came off the road. Selling? No, just dropped off the freights for a while, leaving again tomorrow morning. This your home town? Yes. How far'd you get? The coast. You don't say.
>
> [. . .] Tell me something: How does a fellow eat when he's travelling that way? Back doors. Hm. Can you always get something? Most always, I didn't eat so bad. (CS 110)

Williams' persistent questioning elicits short definitive responses from this wandering workman. His answers reveal his freedom, but also his dependence on the kindness of others—like Williams—for his survival. He appreciates the ride and pays the price of his seat by answering the doctor's questions. He even invites the doctor to come along to a "swimming hole" (111). Although Williams seems uncomfortable extending this relationship beyond the controlled situation of his car, he has made contact with this particular person; and as a result, he has gained some knowledge about the life of the man on the street and managed to recreate his voice.

In terms of the 1913 silk strike, perhaps the most significant aspect of "Life Along the Passaic River" concerns an older resident's recollection of that "bright boy" from Boston, John Reed, and the "big strike at the textile mills" (CS

114). The resident recalls Reed "shooting off his mouth around in the streets here telling us what to do." The tone of the resident's remarks reveals his disgust with Reed:

> Who paid for having their kids and women beat up by the police? Did that guy take a room down on Monroe St. and offer his services for the next ten years at fifty cents a throw to help straighten out the messes he helped get us into? He did not. The Polacks paid for it all. Sure. And raised up sons to be cops too. [. . .] But they ain't moved away none; that's what I'm saying. They're still here. Still as dumb as ever. But it's more than that guy ever give up or could think to do to help them. (CS 114)

This critique of Reed's actions during and after the strike highlights his failure in Paterson. For sure, he brought a lot of attention to the strike through his arrest and his staging of the pageant in New York City. As evident by this Patersonian's recollection, though, his activism had minimal effect on the people who actually worked and lived in Paterson. This resident believes a more practical "service" would have consisted in living, working, and fighting with these workers to change their economic situation. Instead, Reed left Paterson and went off to revolutions occurring in Mexico and Russia. The workers and their children had no choice but to stay. Some of these children even assumed the roles of "cops," who in 1913 "beat up" strikers and were considered the enemy. In the end, the older resident dismisses Reed as a man who became involved not so much to help the plight of workers, but to seek boyish adventure at their expense.

With the heightened talk of Socialism and Communism during the Great Depression, Williams presents the words of an ordinary worker looking back on the ineffectiveness of Reed's radical "shouting" and political art. This reference to the legacy of Reed and the 1913 silk strike shows the staying power of the strike in Williams' imagination. Twenty years later he still appears to be working out a representation of this political "war" in his art. Williams' return to 1913 also reveals a few things. First, it indicates that the socio-economic problems of 1913 persist in contemporary Paterson. Nobody has been able to escape and move away from the city. They have assumed different jobs, but they still remain dominated by their social situation. Second, Williams projects his attitude towards artistic activism through the bitterness of a laborer who experienced the pageantry of 1913. For him, Reed is not a committed revolutionary, but a big talker. Williams once again discounts Reed; this time in regard to the value of his political activities in Paterson. As Whittemore contends, "Reed was brought in as an example of an outsider who would never truly know or understand the local social scene and who should therefore not be regarded as a reliable type to entrust social affairs to" (175).

John Reed also shows Williams what could happen to a poet who became too involved in politics. As previously mentioned, Reed learned that "class struggles play hell with your poetry." He learned that a balance between activism and art was almost impossible. Sherwood Anderson recalled talking with Reed about this subject. Coincidentally, Anderson belonged to "The Friends of William Carlos Williams," a group started by Ford Maddox Ford in 1939. At one point Reed commented to Anderson, "If I could be dead sure I had something on the ball as a poet" (Anderson 183). In another meeting, he showed Anderson some poems and looked like a "pleased boy" because Anderson liked them. He soon left Anderson, however, for the 1917 I.W.W. trial. His departing words were "Well, well, that's enough of this. I guess I'd better get back in there and see what's doing" (183). According to Anderson's memories, Reed's artistic and political desires divided him. At one moment he could discuss the value of his poetry, and in the next moment he could return to the trial of a radical labor organization. In the final assessment, his artistic-political division interfered with his capacity to produce poetry.

Reconciling Political Impulses with Artistic Integrity

Williams understood Reed's struggle to reconcile art with politics. He wanted to be "involved," yet at the same time he resisted a Reed-like immersion that would limit his effectiveness as an artist. An example of his internal struggle occurred in the summer of 1933 when Fred and Betty Miller asked to use his name in connection with their proletarian magazine entitled *Blast*. Interestingly, Fred Miller belonged to the John Reed Club (Weaver 92). The club appealed to "socially conscious" writers and used the slogan "Art is a Class Weapon" (Homberger "Proletarian" 232). Despite his radical ideological affiliation, Miller "could be counted on not to fill his magazine with propaganda" (Weaver 93).

At first, Williams hesitated about getting involved in *Blast*. His hesitation was not because of the magazine's politics, but rather because of the editorial work it involved. The Millers, however, assured Williams that they would handle all the editorial responsibilities. As Mariani suggests, "All they wanted from Williams were some more of those stories they'd read of his [. . .] and a manifesto now and then" (345). Williams agreed to this arrangement. He published several stories in the short-lived magazine (five issues appeared between September 1933 and November 1934): "Jean Beicke," "The Use of Force," "The Dawn of Another Day," "The Girl with a Pimply Face," and a "Night in June." Each of these stories represents incidents in the lives of working-class families. According to Mariani, they "revealed more eloquently than any propaganda could what the economic situation in America had done to thousands of lower-class American families, and how those families had somehow managed to survive [. . .]" (345). These short stories once again show Williams selecting politically charged subjects but refusing to fashion them for ideological ends.

Williams felt the need to clarify his association with *Blast*, so nobody would get the wrong idea. In a statement that was never published, which he wrote for the magazine's first issue, Williams accepts his editorial position on the basis of three crucial criteria:

1. that I have no work to do in connection with it,

2. that it be understood to be and remain a magazine devoted to writing (first and last) though in the service of the proletariat,

3. that it adhere reasonably closely to the following program—(I will write exclusively, consciously and with a purpose to be understood by—and to instruct in the objectives of my craft—those avowed Communists who need what I can give. [. . .])

(RI 75)

Williams' statement reveals his general thoughts about the role of the artist in politics. He asks what a poet should do who is sympathetic to a political cause. He poses the following question: "Shall we give up the essential individualism of artists to serve a proletarian state [. . .] or shall we cling to the drastic compulsions of the artists even at the cost of having the new state excommunicate us?" (77). Repeatedly Williams asserts his belief that the artist should not compromise his or her artistic integrity in service of the party. "He was still interested in one thing and one thing only," as Mariani argues, "to write as well and as honestly as he knew how, and not in the pay of any ideology" (346). Williams wanted to enter and participate in the political arena, yet he wanted to do so on his own terms.

Williams believes that the artist does have a political responsibility. At one point he claims that writers "must face their responsibilities toward the world revolution: to clarify [it] by examples—more effective writing" (RI 75). With his emphasis on effective writing, he aligns the artist's duty with the production of quality art. Disgusted by a tendency of political writers to write down to readers, he argues, "Bad writing never helped anybody. Much proletarian writing is ineffective since it is bad" (75). In effect, Williams' explanation of political responsibility reemphasizes his belief in artistic integrity. Wary of how an ideological purpose degrades art, he speaks out against a Communistic tendency to confiscate and control the artist. According to Williams, an artist mistakenly believes he must dismiss "his personal integrity as an artist" in order "to serve the new mode implied in a present-day Communism" (78). He asserts, "It may be demanded of him—he must deny the demand. His only answer must be, No" (78).

Williams does not totally oppose Communism. He comments that an artist should not take the stand "that Communism as such is opposed to him and that he must dash himself to death against it" (78). Actually, Williams sees some real possibilities for the artist through Communism—in particular, "an opportunity to regain an understanding [. . .]" (78). The artist achieves this understanding by returning to essentials. According to Williams, this return involves "the new stress which Communism places on words and their uses. Communism has cut away whole bales of misconception in form [. . .]" (79). Communism thus allows the artist to evade traditional forms and discover new forms through its stress on basics. In response to a question about the "place of writing in a communistic state," Williams writes,

> My answer is: The same it has always been, only—since there is no remaining objective left to the writer in the forms which have decayed away under his fingers—he must go back for his clue, realistically look for new forms in a more simple organization of social materials. (80)

Significantly, Williams' answer reasserts his conviction about the need for artistic "integrity," yet he also adds that there must be a willingness on the part of the writer to examine the social materials that are available to him. Williams contends that the search through these materials will enable the artist to discover new, basic forms. This call to return to social materials echoes Williams' own search among local materials in the development of his magnum opus *Paterson*. In the end, this search enables him to participate in this proletarian publication.

While Williams worked out the parameters of his participation with proletarian writing, he also participated in the Social Credit Movement that was based upon Major C. H. Douglas's economic theories. This movement attempted to democratize credit by breaking the bankers' control over it. It sought the establishment of a national credit office that would provide credit to people to increase their purchasing power (Weaver 106). The Social Credit Movement, as Weaver remarks, "proposed a greater degree of socialisation without socialism; it was radical without being revolutionary" (107). Williams believed that Social Credit would help end what he perceived as the monopolization of credit and resolve the country's debilitating economic problems. He involved himself on several different levels. He asked speakers to talk to his Polytopics club in Rutherford; he even delivered a speech on the subject at a conference in Charlottesville, Virginia, in July 1936. "Major Douglas and Pound had had a hand in the speech," as Whittemore perceptively notes, "but in the end it was a speech describing WCW's own private movement" (263).

In his speech, Williams argues that the U.S. economic structure subverts the Constitution's "democratic intention." Initially, Americans fought the Revolutionary War for individual liberty. Their democratic ideal, according to Williams, "was not very different from the objective of those advocating a classless society today!" (RI 100). Yet the difficulty of instituting this pure democracy ended up "giving Hamilton his chance" (101), which led to "an industrial autocracy and consequent economic centralization under narrow control." Once again, Williams blames Hamilton for corrupting American democracy. His plan meant that "economic freedom of the individual was a lost cause" (101). Echoing his friend Ezra Pound, Williams recounts the "great battles" that Andrew Jackson and Martin Van Buren fought against Hamilton's Federal Banking system. He calls for the same type of fight in the name of individual economic freedom.

By expressing his desire to reform the credit system, Williams wants to ensure America's capacity to produce rugged individuals. At one point in his speech he asks, "The very type of rugged individual is who? Lenin, Mussolini— and my grandmother" (103). These answers sound strange. First, Williams holds up two such politically charged figures as Lenin and Mussolini to illustrate his point. Considering his book *In the American Grain*, you would expect Williams to present "American" examples of rugged individualism such as Daniel Boone. Secondly, he unexpectedly places his own English grandmother, who served as his muse in "The Wanderer," in the company of these two revolutionary figures. The grouping of the three, with their political and poetic implications, indicates his belief about the need for rugged individuals to stimulate revolutionary change, whether political or poetical.

Williams poses a crucial question in his speech about the future "democratic" direction of the United States:

> shall we extend our present form of government to include the credit situation, making it more and more democratic, or renounce it in favor of some other scheme economically more desirable? Perhaps to the right, perhaps to the left? (RI 98)

At this time, the U.S. is at a crossroad. Although it has the opportunity to realize its democratic premise, it also remains vulnerable to exploitation from other forces. This exploitation may come from either the right or the left—Williams perceives both as real threats. He describes them as "two cures": they may take the form of a "Dictatorship of Labor" or a Fascist control of "the existent dictatorship by the banks" (100). If forced to choose, Williams sides with labor. He claims, "between a stroke for freedom by labor and fascism through Credit Monopoly, what American would not throw in his lot with labor, taking a chance on the result?" (117). Such a preference indicates Williams' sympathy with the plight of the workingman. Yet, although he is sympathetic, he distrusts placing such power in the hands of laborers. He fears the potential for a bloody revolution. The Social Credit Movement thus becomes a way, according to Williams, "[T]o escape these two and retain our present form of government" and "make it fully effective" (100).

The role of the artist is Williams' main focus in his speech. For the benefit of society, artists must retain their freedom to think and to act as they choose. They should be allowed to express their views, whether or not they are in agreement with the "party in power" (106). He presents his own personal struggles to clarify the artist's dilemma. "For the past thirty years," he confesses to the audience, "I have never been able to get one first-rate poem published in a commercial magazine" (107). He admits that he has paid or partially paid for the publication of each of his books. He acknowledges a difference between his poetry and the poetry "commercially published"; he also admits that his work has no market. Williams blames the government for his publishing troubles. As he contends, "I maintain that the quality of individual effort as well as taste is to a large extent the reflection of the government that exists at the time" (108). The monetary value of a book distorts its artistic value. In order to get a book printed and sold, it must, according to Williams, "meet a false standard." This monetary standard corrupts the artist's integrity. After all, as Williams sees it, the artist's job is to

> admit all classes of subject to his attention, even though he hang
> for it. This is his *work*. Nothing poetic in the feudal, aristocratic
> sense but a breaking down, rather, of those imposed tyrannies over
> his verse forms. Technical matters, certainly, but most important
> to an understanding of the poet as a social regenerator. (109)

Clearly, Williams believes that the poet has a duty to write about any subject, irrespective of its social or political appropriateness. He also believes that by breaking down traditional forms an artist will help regenerate society.

At the time, Williams finds Social Credit the most effective plan for resolving America's economic problems. Because it is based upon true respect for individual liberty, Douglas's plan offers the artist a real "opportunity to live" (109). He argues that it "provokes thought, not limits it, buttresses the individual by insuring his economic competence [. . .] relieves him of being subject to the whims of the right or left [. . .]" (113). In contrast to a fascist Credit Monopoly or a proletarian revolution, which would subjugate and discard the artist, the Social Credit Movement offers him real opportunities. It insures economic competence and protection from political control. In defining his position, Williams claims that it is "the only solution that does not depend upon brute force, medieval division of class against class" (111).

Williams' Social Credit speech shows him working out his thoughts about art's relation to politics. His participation in this movement illustrates his desire for social change while at the same time resisting the revolutionary changes proposed by fascists and communists. He wanted to enhance individual liberty and believed that Fascism and Communism threatened this liberty. Just as he does in his *Blast* statement, he asserts the artist's political responsibility at the same time that he champions his artistic integrity.

Williams' ambivalent relationship with the Left also manifests itself in his involvement with two radical magazines—the *New Masses* and the *Partisan Review*. In 1930, he wrote to the *New Masses* for a subscription. In his letter, he states that he is not a Communist because he is first-and-foremost a poet. He concludes, "I'm for you. I'll help as I can. I'd like to see you live" (qtd. in Tashjian 116). His sympathy with the *New Masses* contrasts with his antagonism to the *Partisan Review*. When the *Partisan Review* sent Williams a questionnaire about a symposium entitled "What is Americanism: Marxism and the American Tradition," Williams responded by attacking Marxism. In his response, he praises democracy as a central force that has stood for centuries. He claims,

> [it] has defeated the more radical thought of each era, such as that of Tom Paine, Gene Debs, Bill Haywood, making their movements and thought seem foreign to the environment. It is this same democracy of feeling which will defeat Marxism in America and all other attempts at regimentation of thought and action. It will also defeat fascism [. . .] (SL 157)

Significantly, Williams mentions Bill Haywood as one of these radical forces. As evident with the I.W.W.'s failure in Paterson, his revolutionary labor philosophy did not suit America. In part, Williams suggests, it failed because it was "foreign" to the region; it lacked a true understanding of the local. More startling, however, Williams proclaims—in the pages of the *Partisan Review*—that democracy will defeat Marxism. He continues,

> Marxism is a static philosophy of a hundred years ago which has not yet kept up—as the democratic spirit has—through the stresses of an actual trial. [. . .] It takes a tough theory to survive America, and America thinks it has that theory. Therefore it will smile and suffer [. . .] through all the rottenness, all the political corruption, all the cheap self-interest of its avowedly ruling moneyed class
> [. . .] (SL 157-158)

Here Williams plainly asserts that he is not a Marxist. Despite the many socio-economic problems in contemporary America, he maintains his belief in the viability of democracy. It needs reworking, as he declared in his Social Credit speech, but not a complete overhaul.

In the *Partisan Review's* subsequent issue, the editors called for "Sanctions Against Williams." They claimed that his comments were "roundly condemned by most of the correspondents" and reprinted one letter that thought Williams made "an ass of himself" (30). These sanctions against Williams "amounted to," as Mariani facetiously suggests, "being placed on their list of those to be shot in the coming revolution" (389).

The next year Williams had another run-in with the *Partisan Review*. That fall the *Partisan Review* asked Williams for a poem. He sent them one; they rejected it and asked for another. He then sent "The Defective Record." Again, they rejected his submission and asked for another poem. Williams sent a postcard with the following message: "Your patience will make the flowers bloom" ("Temptation" 61). This submission/ rejection exchange gained significance when Williams announced in the *New Masses* that the *Partisan*

Review would not be receiving a contribution from him.

The editor of *Partisan Review* demanded an explanation from Williams. This explanation appeared with his earlier letters to the *Partisan Review* under the title "The Temptation of Dr. Williams." Here is a portion of Williams' response:

> [. . .] I have no reason for liking the PARTISAN REVIEW. I have, at the same time, no partisan interest in the New Masses. [. . .] As my contribution to the New Masses was of longer standing and of more importance to me than the other and since I found the New Masses violently opposed to you on political grounds, so much so that they refused to print me if I remained a contributor to PARTISAN REVIEW, I made my choice in their favor. (61)

The contribution that Williams mentions is a review of H. H. Lewis's poetry. Williams describes Lewis as "a Missouri farm-hand, first cousin to a mule [. . .]" who was "an instigator to thought about what poetry can and cannot be for us today" (*Poetry* 229). The *Partisan Review* had rejected this review, in part, because a shorter version had already appeared in *Poetry* (Whittemore 256).

Williams' desire to publish his review in the *New Masses*, along with the resulting turmoil it caused with the *Partisan Review*, once again shows his interest in the political magazines as a venue for his writing, but it also demonstrates his unwillingness to swear allegiance to their ideologies. He understood that such an allegiance would limit his freedom as an artist. As Whittemore remarks, "he was trying to be in favor of the poor and against the rich, [. . .] but he was also trying to be, as always, his own man—and that was something he kept discovering the Marxists didn't want him to be" (245).

A Tension Between Poetry and Politics

In "Against the Weather," Williams comments upon the state of "political" poetry:

> I'll back, as I regret, the faces of some of my young compatriots, with scars on their backs and faces, from policeman's fists and clubs, showing the part they have taken in strikes. [. . .] But— when I look at their poems, I wonder. The structure is weak.
>
> (SE 217)

Williams perceived the capacity for political agendas to corrupt poetry. During the 1930s he also struggled in his verse to reconcile his political concerns with his desire for artistic integrity. This artistic-political tension surfaces in *An Early Martyr and Other Poems* (1935). According to Robert von Hallberg, the book tries "to reconcile the political demands of a disruptive decade with the kinds of descriptive and often delicate poetry he was then accustomed to writing" (131). Williams selects a variety of subjects that personify the socio-economic conditions of many Americans. The prevalence of such images caused Mariani to suggest, "he might just as well have called the book *Proletarian Portraits*" (369).

The early martyr of Williams' title is the radical activist John Coffey. A friend of Williams, Coffey fought for social equality in the United States. Williams describes him as "a young radical who wanted to help the poor [. . .]" (IWWP 56). In many ways, Coffey resembles a young John Reed. Coffey came across, as Mariani suggests, "like a true Communist as opposed to the strident leftists who talked and talked and left Williams cold" (358). Coffey's plan involved stealing from department stores, informing the authorities, and then using his trial to gain publicity for the problem of poverty. Like the radical Reed, Coffey understood the importance of media attention. The authorities, however, avoided the publicity of a trial by placing Coffey in an insane asylum. When the asylum became too crowded in the mid 1930s, Coffey was released. In describing Coffey's actions, Williams recalls, "No one at that time would have thought of this as communistic—it was simply an unworldly dream and I was sympathetic to the dreamer and the dream" (IWWP 56). Williams' sympathy for Coffey's "dream" signifies his own desire to overcome the socio-economic divisions he perceived in America society.

Williams pays tribute to Coffey's deeds in "An Early Martyr." The poem begins by recounting Coffey's activities and institutionalization. The unjust system that he fought against remains intact. Yet Williams quickly declares that

> [. . .] his youthful deed
>
> Signalizing
>
> the romantic period
>
> Of a revolt
>
> he served well
>
> Is still good— (CP1 378)

Williams moves beyond pure description in these lines and comments upon the merit of Coffey's revolutionary action. He claims that it could serve as a model for others to follow. He even metaphorically transforms Coffey.

> Let him be
>
> a factory whistle
>
> That keeps blaring—
>
> Sense, sense, sense! (CP1 378)

Williams reverses the meaning of the factory whistle from a call to work to a call for revolution. The repetition of "sense" emphasizes the call's common sense quality. As in some of his poems in *Al Que Quiere!*, Williams dominates the representation of his subject. He instructs his audience about Coffey's importance and becomes the "mind" and "voice" that carries on the dream: "Never give up / keep at it!"

"A Poem for Norman Macleod" is also inspired by one of Williams' radical friends. Williams sympathized with Norman Macleod's desire to break-down class divisions. He tells Thirlwall,

> I was very much in sympathy with Norman Macleod and his social
> attitudes to the poor. I felt that the revolution was coming. I was
> never in favor of the [Communist] Party, but I did think that some
> revolution [would come] which would bring down the socialites
> and give the poor people a chance. (CP1 542)

Reminiscent of his comment in his Social Credit speech, Williams once again
expresses his desire to see social change in favor of the poor.

The poem opens with the declaration that the revolution has been
completed:

> The revolution
>
> is accomplished
>
> noble has been
>
> changed to no bull (CP1 401)

This revolutionary change is epitomized by the poet's transformation of "noble"
into "no bull." He splits the word into its base syllables and discovers a different
meaning. Instead of expressing "noble" sentiments, the poet must impart to his or
her audience "actual" circumstances. As von Hallberg explains, "the revolution
must be based on what is really known, not on bull, and knowledge begins with
the local" (147). True "revolution" demands an understanding of one's local
surroundings. Williams makes this point at the conclusion of his poem:

> You can do lots
>
> if you know
>
> what's around you
>
> No bull (CP1 401)

The vague, conditional assertion that there is "lots" for you to do if you know your
locale, indicates the unlimited possibilities open to a person who makes contact
with his or her locale. Williams, who makes such contact in *Paterson*, ends the
poem by emphasizing his own commitment to the revolution. Although
sympathetic to Coffey and Macleod's revolutionary dreams, he refuses to

subscribe to the party line. Williams has his own ideas about how the artist can overcome the multiple divisions prevalent in American society—"No bull."

Poems like "To a Poor Old Woman" and "Late for Summer Weather" epitomize Williams' local focus—he portrays specific incidents in the lives of poor people. By his focus on the feelings of pleasure and love, Williams tones down the political potential of his subjects. In "To a Poor Old Woman," Williams describes an old woman eating a plum on the street. Although old and poor, this woman manages to find temporary pleasure in the simple act of eating ripe fruit.

> They taste good to her
>
> They taste good
>
> to her. They taste
>
> good to her (CP1 383)

Through his repetition, enjambment, and punctuation (the above period is the only punctuation in the poem), Williams accentuates her sensory pleasure in eating the plums. She has gained momentary "comfort" from her reality of being old and poor.

In "Late for Summer Weather," Williams presents two lovers who are "Fat Lost Ambling / nowhere" (CP1 384). The man wears "an old light grey Fedora" and "a dirty sweater;" the woman wears "an old blue coat / that fits her tight" and "broken down pumps." As evident by their aimless wandering and worn outfits, these two lovers have little more than each other. On their stroll, they kick piles of leaves, which appear as "crisp as dollar bills." Williams' simile highlights the dire economic condition that underlines their stroll. These ragged lovers are literally heading nowhere. The playful kicking of leaves—"Nothing to do. Hot cha!"—emphasizes their attitude towards the situation. Despite a sense of purposelessness, they still manage to find momentary pleasure in their time together. "Emotionally, literally," according to Paul Alec Marsh, "they are living in Indian Summer—on borrowed time—and they know it [. . .]" (358). In both poems, Williams selects poor people but refuses to sermonize about their hardships. Rather, he portrays temporary moments of their delight in living. This approach does two things. It emphasizes their humanity—relating these specific individuals to their broader community. It also dramatizes the constant threat of economic troubles in their lives. Williams thus represents the poor without preaching to his audience.

A more explicit representation of the proletariat's suffering occurs in "The Yachts," which is inspired by the America's Cup yacht races that Williams had seen in Newport, Rhode Island in 1935. Not only does Williams recall the race, but he expresses, as Mariani suggests, "the ambivalence he had felt watching all that aristocratic skill while knowing that it was a nation of poor people who in reality supported this small privileged class" (370). Williams uncharacteristically uses long lines and slant rhymes; these conventions suggest an attempt to relate the dominance of the yachts with traditional, limiting forms of poetic expression. As he comments to Thirlwall, "I was thinking of terza rima, but gave up rime—a *very* vague imitation of Dante. I was quickly carried away by my own feelings" (CP1 541).

Early in the poem Williams describes the yacht race setting:

> brilliance of cloudless days, with broad bellying sails
>
> they glide to the wind tossing green water
>
> from their sharp prows while over them the crew crawls (CP1 388)

Williams projects the grace and power of the race through the alliteration and measure of the lines. Something grotesque, however, underlies the surface. When the wind picks up and the race proceeds, the yachts churn up ghastly images:

> Arms with hands grasping seek to clutch at the prows.
>
> Bodies thrown recklessly in the way are cut aside
>
> It is a sea of faces about them in agony, in despair (CP1 389)

These lines mark a turn in the poem's structure and meaning. "[W]ith the realization that the vehicles of wealth tread on people," von Hallberg remarks, "the rhythm shifts to something more stable, less suspended, as the syntactic units begin to coincide with the line-endings" (141). Symbolizing the inequality inherent in capitalism, this yacht race has a social price tag attached to it. The poet alone perceives this price as the "cries" are "rising / in waves still as the skillful yachts pass over" (CP1 389). By his willingness to look beneath the grace and power of the scene, Williams perceives the class exploitation that underlies the race and thus exposes a system that allows such suffering to continue.

"Proletarian Portrait" is another politically explicit poem. Von Hallberg describes it as a "political parable" (137). Discussing his poem with John Thirlwall, Williams recalls Pound's response: "Ezra Pound wrote that he didn't like this because of the proletarian tone. He thought it was obvious and so what? 'She might have done as well in Russia as in Passaic'" (CP1 540). Obviously from this response, Williams does not share Pound's dislike for his poem's proletarian tone. He does not shy away from its political implications; in fact, he had already changed the title from "Study for a Figure Representing Modern Culture" (CP1 540). According to Dickran Tashjian, "The two titles taken together suggest the tensions Williams felt in trying to reconcile a long-standing split between the avant-garde and the political vanguard on the left" (119).

Williams' poem depicts an ordinary woman on the street. She appears as "[a] big young bareheaded woman / in an apron" (CP1 384). Her bare head and apron reflect an indifference to her working-class status; as von Hallberg suggests, it reveals that she is "uninhibited by bourgeois decorum" (137). Following this description, Williams portrays her action on the street, which further reveals her unabashed social attitude:

> One stockinged foot toeing
> the sidewalk
>
> Her shoe in her hand. Looking
> intently into it

> She pulls out the paper insole
> to find the nail
>
> That has been hurting her (CP1 385)

As she exhibits a determination to confront the problems that oppress her, she represents thousands of workers looking to discover the source of their economic suffering. Such a depiction of a working-class person reflects Williams' approach to representing his political concerns about the proletariat in his art. Like so many of his proletarian portraits, his subject does not speak. He simply represents her as he sees her and thus avoids any social sermons that she may deliver to his readers.

"Sounding Out" About Paterson

While Williams worked to avoid the limitations of "political" art, he continued to develop his thoughts about a poetic expression of the city of Paterson. One expression of these thoughts appears as his 1937 poem "Paterson: Episode 17," which Mariani describes as a "tentative step toward his major poem" (414). Williams' "Paterson: Episode 17" presents his observation of a young African-American maid beating a rug on the lawn of a church.

Williams opens his poem by imaginatively calling out to this young maid: "Beat hell out of it / Beautiful Thing" (CP1 439). His omission of the article creates a gap between "beat" and "hell" that imitates the force of her beat in his verse. Such a device not only emphasizes the sound of her beat, but it expresses the quality of brutality that shapes her life. It also echoes "The Wanderer," where Williams first made the connection between brutality and Paterson. Probing what unites the strikers in his poem "The Wanderer," he asks, "Can it be anything but brutality?" (CP1 31). "Paterson: Episode 17" does not try to depict the brutality that unites a group of Paterson strikers; instead, it focuses on how brutality shapes the life of a solitary woman beating a rug. It represents one answer to the question he asks in "Paterson" (1927), "who are these people?" (CP1 264).

Despite the brutality of this woman's life, Williams calls her "Beautiful Thing." This name reveals Williams' contradictory impulses towards her. Without question, he admires her from afar. Yet his reference to her as a "Thing" is dehumanizing. Later in the poem, he further dehumanizes her by describing her as "some trusting animal" (CP1 440). Although these references suggest Williams' social and racial bias, they also convey society's view of this young African-American woman. After all, as we later see, it is the guys from Newark and Paterson—her hometown—who rape and beat her.

It should also be pointed out, however, that the term "Beautiful Thing" has roots in Williams' earlier work. For example, this phrase appears in "The Discovery of the Indies" from *In the American Grain*. At the conclusion of the essay, Columbus describes the New World as "the most beautiful thing which I had ever seen. [. . .]" (26). The phrase expresses the sense of wonder and awe that comes with the discovery of something new and different. This phrase also refers to the declaration "no ideas but in things" from Williams' poem "Paterson" (CP1 263). The "Beautiful Thing" personifies this poetic credo and the ideas "savage and tender" of "Paterson, that great philosopher—" (263). The name "Beautiful Thing," though it cannot be defined exactly, conveys Williams' wonder and awe of this brutalized figure from Paterson.

It should be noted that the name "Beautiful Thing" also contains the "beat" that is her work and that has shaped her life. Williams describes her work in detail:

> Lift the stick
> above that easy head
> where you sit by the ivied
> church, one arm
> buttressing you

>long fingers spread out
>
>among the clear grass prongs—
>
>and drive it down
>
>Beautiful Thing (CP1 439)

Williams' line breaks slow her actions down to exemplify each aspect of the process, from the lifting to the driving. His description of her body's movement in such detail expresses the powerful sensuality that she holds for him. As the detailed description of her rug beating continues, she assumes sacramental proportions. Her pose is one "of supreme indifference / sacrament / to a summer's day / [. . .] in the unearned suburbs" (440). In her laboring, she stands apart from the suburbs. Williams' choice of the adjective "unearned" to describe the suburbs is curious; it conveys her outsider status. This place of presumed wealth does not seem to deserve the labor of the "Beautiful Thing." Williams' use of the grating "ear / ur" sounds in the phrase emphasizes the tension between this locale and the "Beautiful Thing."

Upon observing her "indifference" and repetitive beating, Williams questions what memories, "what forgotten face," she might be recalling. As a distant observer, he imaginatively fashions her personal history. Through his power as poet, he recreates her forgotten face in the next stanza. He describes, "The incredible / nose straight from the brow" (CP1 440). His line division itself embodies the straightness of that nose. The outward details of her straight nose, "empurpled lips," and "half-sleepy eyes" all contribute to what

>makes a temple
>
>of its place of savage slaughter
>
>revealing
>
>the damaged will incites still
>
>to violence
>
>consummately beautiful thing

Behind this face, Williams discovers a person who has been inwardly beaten as she outwardly beats a rug. Her mind, as Williams' alliteration emphasizes, is a place of "savage slaughter"; his placement of the indented present participle "revealing" offers a bridge to her thoughts as she repetitively beats. Williams represents the "damaged will" with a gap between the words "will" and "incites," yet his consonance unifies the line at the same time. The "Beautiful Thing" embodies contradiction and division.

To open the subsequent stanza, Williams exclaims, "Gently! Gently!" (CP1 440). Within the next few lines, "the fury" awakens. Through her "despair" Williams imaginatively perceives her "story," which he emphasizes "has / no place / to lay its glossy head." In the next stanza "the trick's done," her story unfolds and she appears "drunk and bedraggled" "but not alone! (441).

> The car
>
> > had stopped long since
> >
> > when the others
> >
> > > came and dragged those out
> > >
> > > who had you there (441)

Williams' long indention of "The car" recreates its placement on the margin of "society"; the next line, "had stopped long since," dramatizes the transformation of this transitory machine into a torture chamber where the guys from Newark gang rape the "Beautiful Thing." Alcohol pervades the scene and unloosens the bestial behavior of the men, but it also serves as her "anesthetic":

> Reek of it!
>
> What does it matter?
>
> could set free
>
> only the one thing— (441)

Williams' question interjects a nihilistic tone into the poem—brutality seems the only thing set free. After all, they have taken "the dying swan" in her "white lace dress" and "high heeled slippers." They have brutalized her and taken her innocence and purity.

The "Beautiful Thing" does get released from the car, but there is no romance in her rescue. In fact, her rescuers are just as brutal as her captors.

> And the guys from Paterson
>> beat up
> the guys from Newark and told
> them to stay the hell out
> of their territory and then
> socked you one
>> across the nose
>> Beautiful Thing (441-442)

Williams represents the crudity of this rescue scene in street slang, describing the struggle between the "guys" and their violence against the "Beautiful Thing." His line breaks dramatize the violence that disfigures her. The guys from Paterson gave a "sock" to her nose "for good luck and emphasis / cracking it" (442). Through her disfigurement, the "Beautiful Thing" comes to represent "all / desired women" who have been "marked up / [. . .] for memory's sake / to be credible in their deeds." In other words, her rug beating is not arbitrary and mundane—she knows about "beating" in life.

After this expression of her representative significance, Williams immediately returns to another specific image of the "Beautiful Thing"—"Then back to the party!" (442). Her abuse continues; the others jealously "maled" and "femaled" her. As indicative of his questions, the poet also desires to possess her. The inability to probe further, to clarify the mystery of her life requires greater patience on his part: "It would take / a Dominie to be patient / [. . .] with you—" (442). Still, he lacks a "total" understanding of her.

The next stanza returns to the "Beautiful Thing" as she beats the rug on the church lawn. Williams compares her "flogging" to the

> [. . .] beat of famous lines
> in the few excellent poems

> woven to make you
>
> gracious
>
> and on frequent occasions
>
> foul drunk
>
> Beautiful Thing (CP1 443)

Williams' poem is another attempt to "make" the "Beautiful Thing." Like others, he has tried to capture in the "beat" of his lines the "gracious" and "foul" features of her life. Although he does not quite have his way with her, he understands that she personifies the "pulse of release / to the attentive / and obedient mind." Her resistance to limited, fixed representations pushes him to move beyond poetic conventions in order to discover a form that expresses her true nature.

Williams' imaginative observation of the "Beautiful Thing" enables him to come closer than his previous Paterson poems to expressing the brutality of her life. This brutality, which Williams first described in "The Strike" section of "The Wanderer," constitutes a crucial feature of her experiences. Yet, despite the imaginative unfolding of her brutal memories, Williams remains distant from her and unable to express her voice in his verse.

During his build-up to *Paterson*, Williams did work to recreate the speech he heard around him. The expression of this speech became a key for creating *Paterson*. In the 1938 edition of the *Complete Collected Poems*, a group of four poems appears as "From Paterson"; it includes "At the Bar" and "To Greet a Letter-Carrier." In these two poems, Williams aims to express the American idiom, which he associates with Walt Whitman's innovative use of language ("The American Idiom" 250). Here is "At the Bar":

> Hi, open up a dozen.
>
> Wha'cha tryin' ta do—
>
> charge ya batteries?

Make it two.

Easy girl!
You'll blow a fuse if
ya keep that up. (CP1 457)

His use of short, blunt phrases conveys the familiar feeling of a local bar. Without the constraints of a formal verse structure, he manages to recreate in his lines the unrestrained speech rhythms of this place. "To Greet A Letter-Carrier" also shows Williams experimenting with colloquial expression:

Why'n't you bring me
a good letter? One with
lots of money in it.
I could make use of that.
Atta boy! Atta boy! (CP1 458)

Williams' playfully questions the mailman about a common complaint of many people—no good mail. He conflates the phrase "Why didn't" into one sound and concludes with a conflation and repetition of the phrase: "That's it boy" into "Atta boy." Again, he conveys a degree of familiarity and ease. Both of these poems illustrate Williams' break from strict measures and forms in an effort to express the speech that he heard around him.

Williams also sent an 87-page typescript entitled *Detail & Parody for the poem Paterson* to his publisher James Laughlin in 1939 (CP1 547). Part of the *Detail & Parody*, appeared in *The Broken Span* in 1941 as a sequence of fifteen poems entitled "For the Poem Patterson." Several of these poems further demonstrate Williams' experimentation with the American idiom. Here is one of the details:

Doc, I bin lookin' for you
I owe you two bucks.
How you doin'?

> Fine. When I get it
>
> I'll bring it up to you. (CP2 20-21)

Williams takes these words from his personal experience as a physician. Through these short colloquial phrases, he recreates a brief conversation with a patient. Despite the awkwardness of the money matter, the patient's familiarity with the "Doc" reflects an implicit understanding between these two men about the unstated financial trouble. In a note to an earlier version of the detail, Williams explains his purpose in these lines:

> This is the sort of thing, in its essential poetic nature, it's [sic] rhythmic make up (analyzed) [of which] the poetry I want to write is made. The reason I haven't gone on with *Paterson* is that I am not able to—as yet, if ever I shall be. It must be made up of such *speech* (analyzed). (qtd. in Fiero 974)

According to Fiero, "Directly caught live speech gives Williams immediacy of contact with his subject; more than this, it presents a counter voice that often arrests and sometimes ironically complicates the poet's private contemplations" (974). Williams' creation of these details and many other short idiomatic poems are thus significant steps in his development toward *Paterson*.

During World War II, Williams continued to struggle with a form for his epic. In one letter to his publisher James Laughlin, he exclaims, "*Paterson*, I know, is crying to be written, the time demands it [. . .]" (WCW/JL 83). In another letter he writes, "That God damned and I mean God damned poem *Paterson* has me down. I am burned up to do it but don't quite know how" (95). In April 1943, Williams published in *View* "Paterson: The Falls." This poem represents the "late stages" of Williams' thoughts about the form for his epic. It opens with a question that had troubled Williams since 1913 when he first tried representing the striking silk workers of Paterson.

> What common language to unravel?

> The Falls, combed into straight lines
> from that rafter of a rock's
> lip. Strike in! the middle of

> some trenchant phrase, some
> well packed clause. Then . . . (CP2 57)

As a poet attempting to represent his locale, Williams must unravel the language of this place. His exclamatory phrase "Strike in!" echoes the genesis of Paterson—the section of "The Wanderer" entitled "Paterson—The Strike." It also illustrates the type of force that will be needed for him to express this language.

"Paterson: The Falls" offers a rough outline for *Paterson*. Williams fills the gap of the previous unfinished sentence with a clear, direct statement about the structure of his "magnum opus": "This is my plan. 4 sections: First, / the archaic persons of the drama." He announces *Paterson's* four book structure and indicates that he will first introduce the archaic persons of the epic, who appear in Book I as a male—the city of Paterson—and a female—Garret Mountain and the surrounding natural landscape. After stating the plan, Williams begins to unravel the multiple voices inherent in the roar of the Passaic Falls. One of the "wild" voices comes from "the shirt-sleeved / Evangelist" who appears in *Paterson* Book II as Klaus Ehrens. He proclaims, "I am the Resurrection / and the Life!" (CP2 58).

With Ehrens's voice still "echoing" in his mind, Williams describes the third section: "Third, the old town: Alexander Hamilton" (58). Masterfully, Williams coordinates Hamilton and the establishment of the city. He describes Hamilton as

> [. . .] stopped cold
> by that unmoving roar, fastened
> there: the rocks silent

> but the water, married to the stone,
>
> voluble, though frozen; the water
>
> even when and though frozen
>
> still whispers and moans—

Both Hamilton and the Passaic Falls are "stopped cold" in this moment of contact. The Falls will never be the same following Hamilton's vision; Williams makes this evident in the "whispers and moans" that emanate from the frozen water. In the next stanza, he expresses the result of this coming together through sound— "a factory bell clangs, at dawn." This industrial transformation of the place sets-up the final section: "Fourth, / the modern town, a / disembodied roar!" This roar expresses the dislocation of language from the locale. Fragmentation is evident in "the cataract and / its clamor broken apart" (CP2 58). The sound has been divorced from its natural origins. There is a stripping down to basics—a departure "from all learning." Through this process there emerges an unfiltered experience of sound—"the empty / ear struck from within, roaring [. . .]" Williams' ellipses leave this short blueprint open-ended, just like the epic that he eventually develops beyond four books.

From his publication of "The Wanderer" in 1914 to the 1944 poem "Paterson: The Falls," Williams continually returned to the city of Paterson as a subject for his poetry. Although at times he experienced frustration about his representation of the people and their speech, each attempt moved him closer to the development of his long poem. Throughout this period, Williams also made use of the social materials available to him as an artist. Despite his interest in the social problems of the era, particularly in the plight of the working class, Williams resisted submitting his skills to the service of any ideology. He wanted to participate in social movements and contribute to political dialogues, but he refused to write poetry that promulgated an ideological message. In this way, Williams retained the artistic freedom that enabled him to "listen clearer" to the speech of his locale and "sound out" the form of his finest achievement: *Paterson*.

CHAPTER 5

WEAVING TOGETHER THE THREADS OF *PATERSON*

The danger in a study that examines William Carlos Williams' use of the volatile labor history related to Paterson is to pull too hard at a particular thread, reduce the poem to historical analysis or a social sermon, and thus unravel the artistry that is *Paterson*. Instead of trying to impose a fixed meaning on *Paterson*, my purpose in this chapter is to examine the specific references so important to this study: the 1913 silk strike, "The Wanderer," and several key historical figures—John Reed, Catholina Lambert, and Alexander Hamilton. Through an examination of how Williams weaves these particular elements into the poem, one will ascertain their importance in the tapestry that is *Paterson*.

In "Caviar and Bread Again," Williams claims that it is the poet's duty to "lead" the race when it has "gone astray" (SE 102). This duty demands that the poet organize the "materials his age has placed before him" and invent a technique (103). In *Paterson*, Williams attempts to use the local materials available to him to create a poem expressive of his modern age. When asked by John Thirlwall if the 1913 strike, one of these local "materials," centered his interest on *Paterson*, Williams responded:

> Well, it didn't particularly focus my attention, but it was a more

> general attention. I wanted to get an image, an image which
> concerns all men, and yet a noble image. And the image of a city
> was necessary for me, the city of Paterson was most convenient.
> (308)

Williams' ambiguous response does not clearly identify the strike as the seed of his epic poem, but it does suggest that, in the very least, the struggle of the striking workers helped to draw his attention to the potential of his locale to represent his modern age.

The publication of *Paterson* Book I in 1946 signaled the maturation of a poem that Williams had struggled to write for over thirty years. As a sensitive observer, Williams perceived the troubling divisions prevalent throughout modern American society. Early in Section ii of *Paterson* Book I, he exclaims, "Divorce is / the sign of knowledge in our time, / divorce! divorce!" (P 17). In response to this sense of divorce, Williams searches for a "redeeming language" that will bring unity and harmony to this place and its people. In a 1951 note to *Paterson* he writes,

> The noise of the Falls seemed to me to be a language which we
> were and are seeking and my search, as I looked about, became to
> struggle to interpret and use this language. This is the substance of
> the poem. (xiv)

Integral to his search, Williams explores the city's industrial history, including the 1913 strike that dramatically exposed the severe social divisions of Paterson. In "The Wanderer," Williams witnessed these troubling divisions and saw the need for the poet to lead a people "gone astray" (SE 102). He felt as if he had "failed" the strikers by his inability to comprehend the speech of the place. Despite his sense of failure, Williams was deeply affected by the unity of the strikers and their fight against the established power structure of the silk manufacturers—"It sank deep into the blood, that I rose upon / The tense air enjoying the dusty fight" (CP1 31). The tension and conflict of this place demanded his attention. He understood that if he was to discover a redeeming language, he needed to move beyond a conventional poetic language and stereotypical representation. Like the 1913 silk strikers he portrayed in his poem, Williams sought a way to break free from a restrictive, limiting structure. He needed to find a medium, as John Reed did with the Paterson Pageant, which would allow this place and its people to tell their story. His experiments resulted in *Paterson*. Through his innovative juxtaposition of poetry and prose, Williams creates a poem that refuses to be restricted to a singular, authoritative voice. In contrast to his failure to express the speech of this place in 1913, Williams' multi-genre poem seeks to recreate the multiple voices of Paterson and thus express the language of the place.

Getting Started

The Preface to *Paterson* introduces Williams' dilemma as an American poet. He begins by declaring: "Rigor of beauty is the quest. But how will you find beauty when / it is locked in the mind past all remonstrance?" (3). The search for a beauty that seems beyond expression presents the poet with a serious challenge. His response to this perplexing question is sudden and immediate—he will start out small:

> To make a start,
>
> out of particulars,
>
> and make them general, rolling
>
> up the sum, by defective means— (3)

Williams' use of these short lines dramatizes his intent to focus on the disparate "things" that constitute Paterson. He understands the imperfect nature of his method, but he cannot turn away. He describes himself as "just another dog / among a lot of dogs." Others, like Pound, simply "run out— / after the rabbits" and avoid the challenge presented by their native land. As a lame dog with only three legs, he remains alone to "Dig / a musty bone." His digging, his immediate contact, ultimately results in his "interpenetration" with this place and the formation of an identity—"the city, / the man" (4). Through the continual process of "rolling up" opposites, the "obverse, reverse; the drunk the sober; the illustrious / the gross," the poet "[r]enews himself" and makes his way "to Paterson" (4; 5).

Returning to his own poetic past, Williams weaves lines from "Paterson" into his epic. Nancy Barry suggests that Williams uses his earlier poems in an effort "to escape the historical moment of his own writing" ("Epic" 2). During his mythic description of Paterson in Book I, "The Delineaments of the Giants," he inserts the line—"Say it, no ideas but in things" (P 6). This line invokes his earlier attempt to overcome the divisions evident in this place. This phrase is not the only line from "Paterson" to appear in *Paterson*. Williams also interlaces the lines describing the river "pouring in above the city" (7), Paterson's "thoughts sitting and standing" in the bus (9), and his desire to know the people who "walk incommunicado" (10).

The reappearance of these lines reflects Williams' progressive conception of *Paterson*. Similar to his 1920s experimentation in works like *The Great American Novel* and *In the American Grain*, Williams integrates the past into the present moment of writing. He resists a closed reading of Paterson's history. As he exclaims in "The Virtue of History," "History must stay open, it is all humanity" (IAG 189). Williams destroys a fixed, limiting expression of Paterson by juxtaposing different forms of writing (poetry and prose) and different periods of writing (past and present). This destruction of a constrictive form is crucial for his poetic quest. As Brian Bremen contends, "Williams needs to use violence if he is to begin to *change* history. [. . .] Freeing the language, freeing the beauty ... always takes place through violence in Williams [. . .]" (36). Williams learned this lesson as early as 1913 when he portrayed the strikers' "dusty fight" against an oppressive socio-economic structure.

The state of being "incommunicado" that Williams portrays among the people in the city is reminiscent of the strikers' silence in "The Wanderer." In *Paterson*, this linguistic stasis has severe consequences, for "they die also /

incommunicado" (P 11). Williams exclaims,

> The language, the language
>
> fails them
>
> They do not know the words
>
> or have not
>
> the courage to use them   . (11)

Two historical figures epitomize the severity of this linguistic failure: Mrs. Sarah Cumming and Sam Patch, who is also known as Noah Faitoute Paterson. Mrs. Cumming fell or deliberately jumped to her death in the Passaic Falls in June 1812. On the other hand, Patch, a former supervisor of cotton spinners, made a career out of jumping into the Passaic Falls. When he died jumping into the Genesee River, Williams mentions that he lost his capacity to speak: "Speech had failed him. He was confused. The word had been drained of its meaning" (P 16). Both Mrs. Cumming and Patch met their deaths in the tumult of the Passaic Falls and this contact silenced them. "The voiceless drownings of Sam Patch [. . .] and Mrs. Cumming," according to James E. Miller, "offer a paradigm for a languageless, perishing America, suffering from 'blockage' [. . .] and from 'divorce,' a failure of connecting humanly because of a failure of language" (143).

In Section i, Williams also introduces the effect of Alexander Hamilton's industrial vision on the city of Paterson. He presents a prose passage that describes the transformation of Paterson after Hamilton "looked (at the falls!) and kept his counsel" (P 10). Since Hamilton first viewed the place, "the mills had drawn a heterogeneous population" that included French, German, English, Irish, Scotch, Hollanders, and Swiss. These diverse people were attracted to this place to make money. One of these immigrants was "(Mr. Lambert who later built the Castle among them)." Although a poor laborer upon his arrival in America, Catholina Lambert made himself into one of Paterson's wealthiest silk manufacturers. He then built a Castle, Belle Vista, on his mountain property. Despite his working-class roots, Lambert had little sympathy for the laboring class and took a hardline position during the 1913 strike. With this reference to Hamilton and Lambert, Williams introduces the impact industrialization and capitalism has had on the fragmentation of this place. Immediately after this passage, the Falls turn more tumultuous: "Around the falling waters the Furies hurl! / Violence gathers, spins in their heads summoning / them" (P 10).

Williams' unfavorable depiction of industrialization led Babette Deutsch to ask him about his representation of labor violence in *Paterson*. He tells her that there is little he wants "to say about labor violence" in the city of Paterson and directs her to "The Strike" section in "The Wanderer" and "Life Along the Passaic River" (SL 258). He then mentions that in Book I of *Paterson*

> the social unrest that occasions all strikes is strong—underscored,
> especially in the 3rd part, but I must confess that the aesthetic
> shock occasioned by the rise of the masses upon the artist receives
> top notice. (258-259)

The masses have the potential power to destroy the established order of things. As a middle-class artist interested in destroying restrictive forms, Williams considers such revolutionary action shocking—for the possibility of liberation and destruction is one.

In the third section of Book I, Williams relates industry's corruption of this place—he specifically portrays how the dyeing companies have polluted the river and perverted the idyllic beauty of the Passaic Falls.

> Half the river red, half steaming purple
> from the factory vents, spewed out hot,
> swirling, bubbling. The dead bank,
> shining mud . (P 36)

The colorful dyes have transformed the river into a simmering cauldron and killed its bank. As evident by "the ravished park," which Paterson attributes to the "wild workers' children tearing up the grass," this degradation and simmering volatility has spread to the city and its people. Paterson thinks about the crudity of "their mouths eating and kissing, / spitting and sucking, speaking" (36). These distasteful thoughts interfere with his desire to identify with the people. Yet there is little he can do to avoid them. After all, the "silk spins from the hot drums to a music / of pathetic souvenirs [. . .] / to / remind him, to remind him!" He even recalls an old friend's (Pound's) criticism of his poetic focus: "Your interest is in the bloody loam but what / I'm after is the finished product" (37). This reminder of his interest in the "actual" drives Paterson's thoughts out to the suburbs, but he gains no solace there. He finds the red brick of a convent irritating; the simile "red as poor-man's flesh" offers another reminder of the red river, the working class, and revolution.

His thoughts return to the tenements and the "vulgar streets" (38). He perceives the social unrest of the place. The blood of the people here, like the red dye in the river, is "boiling as though in a vat." Despite his disgust with "[p]laster saints" and "rancid meat," he still has the ability to perceive a "forthright beauty" and "loveliness" in this place. Stephen Tapscott offers a sound explanation of Paterson's capacity to see beauty here:

> Sometimes the things of the world hold their beauty only in potential, because the political and economic conditions of entrepreneurial capitalism have exploited or stultified the energies of the natural world. In such conditions, language must try to bridge between the internal beauty "locked in the mind" and the squalid objective "thing." (211)

Paterson thus looks past these "things unmentionable" (P 38), which signify the socio-economic problems of the region, and perceives "(in his thoughts)" the potential beauty of the place.

"The Wanderer" and the Working Class of Paterson

In his letter to Deutsch, Williams also mentions that he would be treating the subject of labor unrest in Book II of *Paterson*. He remarks that there will be much more

> relating to the economic distress occasioned by human greed and
> blindness—aided, as always, by the church, all churches in the
> broadest sense of that designation—but still, there will be little
> treating directly of the rise of labor as a named force. I am not a
> Marxian. (SL 259)

Williams again demonstrates his sensitivity to ideological interpretations of his work. His purpose in *Paterson* is not to sermonize about the plight of labor. His comment, however, does express his determination to portray the forces—industry and religion—that have fostered social inequality in a city like Paterson. In the context of his letter to Deutsch, Williams' interest in an event like the 1913 strike would not reside in the specific incidents of violence that occurred, but rather the contributing factors that led workers to unify and oppose manufacturers.

Book II, "Sunday in the Park," makes a deliberate connection to the 1913 silk strike through excerpts from "The Wanderer." Williams had difficulty writing Book II. At one point in the drafting process, as Nancy Barry notes, he included two pages from "The Strike" section of "The Wanderer." She asserts that "seeing its pages woven into the manuscripts for Book Two, the poem projects both style and form onto the later epic . . ." ("Fading" 347). Williams' use of "The Wanderer" is apparent in Paterson's walk through the park, which echoes the young poet's wandering through the city. Like that earlier figure, Paterson observes the working class. To describe the young women and men he sees, Williams uses lines from the "Paterson—The Strike" section:

> .   . the ugly legs of the young girls,
> pistons too powerful for delicacy!   .
> the men's arms, red, used to heat and cold,
> to toss quartered beeves and   . (P 44)

His use of this excerpt establishes a direct connection between the 1913 strikers and these idle workers. The reappearance of this charged physical description emphasizes the impact of industry on them. Despite the time change, they continue to be shaped by the rigors of their labor. "The people we hear and see are full of a crude animal vitality," as John Johnston explains, "but the conditions of life in an industrial society have vulgarized and degraded them; their minds and souls—and even their bodies—are debased" (216). The reappearance of these lines from "The Strike" indicates that this industrial degradation has occurred for generations.

As Paterson climbs the mountain with the working men and women, he looks back upon the ground they have traversed. What he and the others have passed beyond is the imposing presence of Catholina Lambert's Castle:

> Arrived breathless, after a hard climb he,
>
> looks back (beautiful but expensive!) to
>
> the pearl-grey towers! Re-turns
>
> and starts, possessive, through the trees, (P 44)

The parenthetical remark expresses Williams' ambivalent response to the structure—his appreciation of its beauty and his understanding of its cost. The entire castle, according to one estimate, cost "more than half-a-million dollars" (Alaya 12). This representation of aristocratic opulence literally came at the expense of the mill workers' labor and stood as a formidable marker of the socio-economic gap in Paterson. The struggle involved with climbing past this structure, as reflected in the forced pauses in the lines, indicates the oppressive force that Paterson and these workers have tried to leave behind, if only for an afternoon.

Later in the section, Williams includes a prose passage recounting how in 1880 the German Singing Society of Paterson turned from festive singers "into an infuriated mob" because William Dalzell shot John Joseph Van Houten for trespassing (P 46). The significance of this incident illustrates the latent power of the masses. By inserting into the passage Hamilton's derogatory reference to the masses as "a great beast," Williams expresses the volatile divisions present in

American society. According to Benjamin Sankey, "The incident illustrates a dialectic—people vs. property owner—that operates in several key passages, for instance in the story of Lambert . [. . .] Dalzell, like Lambert, appears as one man fighting for his property rights against the mass [. . .]" (76). Not only does this passage relate to the potential violence of the working class and further develop the theme of social unrest in *Paterson*, but it also foreshadows Lambert's struggle in 1913 with the forces of labor in Book III.

Paterson feels both attracted to the people and distant from them during his wandering on Garret Mountain. As noted previously, Williams had tremendous sympathy and compassion for the working people of Paterson. "His natural sympathy for the common man," according to John Thirlwall, "wells up strong in *Book II* of *Paterson* [. . .]" (276). Despite this sympathy, however, Williams had difficulty bridging the gap to the workers. As Robert Cole remarks, Williams was "aware that he had always been, from birth on, all things considered, a singularly blessed animal (socially, economically) rather than an anonymous cell of the 'great beast'" (222). This difference is dramatically apparent when he first observed the silk strikers in "The Wanderer." He knows that his artistic life contributes to this difference: "they respect me, not as a doctor, but because of this world which they don't understand [. . .] So I must make it apparent to them" (Thirlwall 277). This paternalistic attitude further reflects Williams' distance from the people. In *Paterson*, however, he refuses to turn away—"to escape from the scene would be a defeat for me." He struggles to overcome his sense of distance, as he explains, by placing himself as "a part of the scene." Although his distance continues to frustrate him at points in the poem, Williams' unceasing desire to bridge the gap between himself and the working people results in his "descent" in Book III and his more sensitive understanding of the brutalized "Beautiful Thing."

Farther on in his walk, after he "leaves the path" (P 47), Paterson comes across two young lovers lying semi-naked under a bush. They appear to him "beneath // the sun in frank vulgarity," yet they are "[n]ot undignified" (51). This public display of sexuality and love personifies Williams' complicated response to the working class. He disrupts his detailed description with a general declaration:

> Minds beaten thin
>
> by waste—among
>
>
> the working classes SOME sort
>
> of breakdown
>
> has occurred. [. . .] (51)

These young lovers embody the cultural breakdown evident in this place. They are products of the socio-economic waste surrounding them. As in the earlier description of the strikers on the bread-line, these young lovers also have been brutalized by their environment. Williams' capitalization and pun on SOME/ S.U.M. alludes to the force responsible for this social breakdown.

Despite their crudeness, these lovers do speak to one another. There is "talking, flagrant beyond all talk" (51). They manage to communicate to one another, even though their minds are beaten thin by waste. Williams relates how "their pitiful thoughts do meet // in the flesh—surrounded by churring loves!" (52). They have found a way to express their love, and Williams in turn has found a way to express them in his verse. This passage was crucial for Williams:

> I was always concerned with the plight of the young in the industrial age who are affected by love. [. . .] I love the impassioned simplicity of young lovers. When it's thwarted, and they don't know it's thwarted, then the vulgarity is lifted to distinction by being treated with the very greatest in art which I can conceive. It's easy to miss, but the whole theme of *Paterson* is brought out in this passage, the contrast between the mythic beauty of the Falls and Mountain and the industrial hideousness. But they haven't been able to lick us. [. . .] I will not be licked; so in this

> scene love has triumphed. (Thirlwall 276-277)

Williams is drawn to the natural expression of love and disgusted by its corruption. He refuses to turn away from the "frank vulgarity" he witnesses and manages to find hope in this "[n]ot undignified" union—the triumph of love—that can overcome the social breakdown inherent in this place, if only temporarily (P 51).

Paterson continues walking and soon "rejoins the path" (P 52). He comes upon a stone bench where a man grooms his dog. Like the poet seeking to "comb out the language" (145), this man "is combing out a new-washed Collie bitch" (53). From this place, he looks around:

> .   to the right
>
> from this vantage, the observation tower
>
> in the middle distance stands up prominently
>
> from its pubic grove

The tower offers another representative image of Lambert's power over the land. Lambert built this tower in 1896; it was a place where he showed his guests "the most splendid views in all of North Jersey" (Alaya 12). From such a tower, Lambert could claim visual ownership over all he surveyed.

Despite the tower's presence, "still the picnickers come on" (P 54). They are used to living under such forms of power. Paterson does not turn away from the tower or the noise of "The 'great beast' come to sun himself." The voices of the people are "multiple and inarticulate." He listens to the rhythms of their speech and "strains to catch / the movement of one voice among the rest" (54). Williams recalled to Thirlwall, "I went on Sundays in summer when the people were using the park, and I listened to their conversation as much as I could" (308).

From this spot, Paterson surveys all that lies below the mountaintop. Of particular note, he sees "the church / spires" and "beyond the gap where the river / plunges into the narrow gorge" (P 55). Following this "unseen" plunge, the "imagination soars" and once again he hears that "thundrous" and "endless" voice of the Falls. He describes the power of a voice

> that has ineluctably called them—

>> that unmoving roar!

> churches and factories

>> (at a price)

> together, summoned them from the pit .

The "thundrous voice" that has caused his imagination to soar is the same one that has enticed the forces of industry and religion to establish themselves in this region. His parenthetical remark notes the costly impact of these forces on this place and its people.

Paterson wanders through the crowd—"his voice mingling with other voices" (56). He hears the working people singing and observes them drinking, dancing, and relaxing. One particular woman, Mary, captures his attention when she gets up and dances:

>> La la la la!

> What a bunch of bums! Afraid somebody see

> you?

>> Blah!

>>> *Excrementi!*

>>> —she spits.

> Look a' me, Grandma! Everybody too damn

> lazy. (P 57)

Williams' spacing of lines and colloquial phrases recreate the rhythm of Mary's remarks. Her taunts, crude declarations, and exclamations demonstrate her exuberant vitality. Her words and dance suggest the expressive potential of the place. She transcends the particular contemporary scene: "This is the old, the very old, old upon old, / the undying [. . .]" (57). In contrast to the silent strikers in "The Wanderer" and the incommunicado in "Paterson," Williams' presentation of Mary's spirited voice indicates his progress towards an actual expression of the people he seeks to make contact with in Paterson.

The next section examines the socio-economic structure responsible for the social breakdown that Paterson has witnessed. Early in the section, Williams includes a statement that the church is all the poor have in this world. It turns the poor people's attention from material needs to spiritual rewards. Following his statement about the church, Williams declares that "Cash is mulct of them that others may live / secure / . . and knowledge restricted" (62). The hoarding of cash ensures the current power structure, at the expense of economic and intellectual equality. After linking the forces of religion and capitalism, Williams presents a portion of a letter, which is most likely written by his friend Fred Miller from *Blast* (Weaver 207). The excerpt describes the Senate's attempt to award "the bomb" to industrialists and criticizes its communist scare tactics (P 62). The letter concludes by asking, "are Communists any *worse* than/ the guilty bastards trying in that way to undermine us?" Williams' juxtaposition of these declarations establishes his theme of economic distress fostered by religion and capitalism. He identifies the dangers of monopolies, as Peter Schmidt suggests, that "control the means of production and distribution [. . .] whether they involve the tangible goods of politics and economics or the intangible 'good' of religion and art" (196). In place of this absolute control, Williams prefers, according to Schmidt, "a more 'natural' form of organization—*many* sources of production and no control of the rights of distribution."

Paterson, also referred to as Noah Faitoute, eventually comes upon the evangelist Klaus Ehrens preaching to a small congregation. Significantly, Ehrens preaches close to Lambert's observation tower: "a / cramped arena has been left clear at the base / of the observation tower near the urinals" (P 63). Ehrens' location at the base of Lambert's tower further aligns capital and religion (though not favorable to religion as evident by Ehrens' placement near the urinals). Ehrens places a few children on benches to attract others, yet "his decoys bring in no ducks" (65). Part of Ehrens' problem, according to Margaret Glynne Lloyd, concerns "his inadequate language and consequent inability to relate to his following [. . .]" (219). Only Paterson stands and listens. He hears Ehrens' life story: his rise from "rags to riches," his emigration to America, and his conversion to Christianity.

Prior to his presentation of Ehrens' sermon, Williams places an excerpt of a letter from Marcia Nardi. Nardi was a struggling poet who turned to Williams for poetic and financial assistance; she came away deeply disappointed with his response to her. Several excerpts from her letters appear throughout *Paterson* and give expression to a blunt, critical female voice. In this excerpt, she admits that her failure to communicate with him has had a "disastrous" effect upon her (P 64). Rather than attempt such "*complete* self-honesty" again, she prefers, as she states, to be "entirely misunderstood and misjudged in all my economic and social maladjustments [. . .]." This letter provides a preface to Ehrens' sermon and introduces the problem of ineffective communication that surfaces in this section.

To dramatize how the church aids industry, Williams weaves together Ehrens' preaching about spiritual wealth and Hamilton's vision for material wealth. For example, he interjects into Ehrens' account of his former riches a prose passage describing how Alexander Hamilton assumed control over the United States. Hamilton "saw more clearly than anyone else" the need for a strong Federal government (P 67). After Ehrens tells how he came to America, Williams includes another excerpt about Hamilton, specifically regarding his "Assumption" plan. The passage refers to Hamilton's "vigor and cunning" for instituting a plan that would empower the Federal government. By offsetting Ehrens' ineffective preaching with an historical account of Hamilton's shrewdness, Williams interlaces the past into the bleak contemporary situation. "The juxtaposition of this material," according to Lloyd, "reveals the underlying pathos and tragedy of the inhabitants of Paterson, who have not only suffered from the completion of Hamilton's plans but who also lack any viable contemporary leadership or hope [. . .]" (216).

Upon his arrival in America, Ehrens discovered that he was "a pretty small frog in a mighty big pool" and again had to work hard to make money (P 67). The wealth he generated, however, did not make him happy or "GOOD" (68). Immediately after Ehrens' confession of greed, Williams presents a hymn to American avarice entitled "America the golden!," which is a parody of "America the Beautiful."

> America the golden!
> with trick and money
> damned
> like Altgeld sick
> and molden
> we love thee bitter
> land
>
> Like Altgeld on the
> corner
> seeing the mourners
> pass
> we bow our heads
> before thee
> and take our hats
> in hand (68)

Williams' parody alludes to the Governor of Illinois John Peter Altgeld (1892-1896) who pardoned several people connected to the Haymarket Riots. Altgeld also refused to call out the National Guard for employers during the Pullman Strike (Weaver 208). The Altgeld allusion invokes two incidents that expose the violent potential of the working class towards its employers. Following Ehrens' confession of avarice, this hymn expresses Williams' bitterness over a culture that promises beauty but engenders economic and social inequality. "Williams is likening himself (and 'us')," according to Joel Conarroe, "to a man sickened by death brought about by economic chaos in a 'money grubbing such as I knew and violently wrote against'" (123).

It took a visit from the Lord for Ehrens to turn from his riches. The Lord said, "Klaus, get rid of your / money. You'll never be happy until you do that" (P 69). After this divine command, Williams places a prose excerpt describing Hamilton's desire for the Federal government to make money through industrialization. This money making plan is linked to Hamilton's vision of the Passaic Falls: "His fertile imagination envisioned a great manufacturing center, a great Federal City, to supply the needs of the country" (70). Instead of seeing the mythic beauty of the place, Hamilton imposed his grand scheme upon the scene to create "a national manufactury" (70). The juxtaposition of Hamilton's plan and Ehrens' sermon present the two messages—accumulation of wealth; and peace through poverty—that have generated the "economic distress" Williams mentioned in his letter to Deutsch. While he continues to listen to Ehrens, Paterson thinks about the 1850 hanging of John Johnson who murdered an elderly couple to steal their money. Paterson notes, "From here, one could see him . . . being hanged" (72). The visualization of this hanging dramatizes the deadly effect of America's monetary focus. According to Conarroe, "Williams finds him [John Johnson] no more guilty than those who restrict knowledge, mulct cash, or batten off interest charges, for these things too rob man of his life" (123).

Once Ehrens' sermon concludes, Williams weaves into his verse prose passages critical of the Federal Reserve System, which issues and regulates the distribution of money. The first excerpt charges that "[t]he Federal Reserve System is a private enterprise [. . .] a private monopoly [. . .] (with power) [. . .] given to it by a spineless Congress [. . .] to issue and regulate all our money" (P 73). This passage and the others come from a sheet produced by Alfredo and Clara Studer (P 273). Since the excerpts appear after what Williams describes as "the preacher's clownish talk" (273), Charles Doyle suggests that it "offers the possibility that he saw the matter of the leaflet as a *practical* alternative to the preacher's exhortations" (109).

Another prose excerpt in this section recounts Hamilton's organization of S.U.M., which took control of the area and transformed Hamilton's vision of the Falls into a reality. It tried implementing L'Enfant's "magnificent" design for the city, but in the end utilized Peter Colt's more "practical" plan (P 74). William Sharpe interprets the danger of such planning on the region:

> the town planners attempted to impose order upon the uneven terrain of Paterson [. . .] But to dedicate any society to rigid structures is to alienate it from the landscape that gives it life [. . .]
> (146)

S.U.M.'s plan thus violated the locale. It imposed order instead of comprehending the nature of the place. Since S.U.M. initiated its plans, this place "has undergone / a subtle transformation, its identity altered" (P 18). As Joseph Riddel remarks, "the modern city is the testimony to Hamilton's design, the systematic imposition of reason to channel power, the tyranny of reason [. . .]" (160).

Williams dramatizes S.U.M.'s impact on the new nation with a description of George Washington wearing "a coat of Crow-black homespun woven / in Paterson" at his first inaugural (P 74). This loaded image of Washington cloaked in a Paterson product represents the extent of Hamilton's power. In contrast to this powerful image, Williams places an excerpt from "Tom Edison on the Money Subject" (74). The passage describes the Federal Reserve Bank as a "Legalized National Usury System" whose primary customer is the Government. It criticizes bonds and interest charges and claims, "If the people ever get to thinking of bonds and bills at the same time, the game is up." The placement of this passage after the Washington image conveys the simmering volatility underlying America's economic system.

After witnessing Ehrens' failure to offer a viable message to the people, Williams questions the wisdom of his continued digging in this place. He asks,

> Why should I move from this place
>
> where I was born? knowing
>
> how futile would be the search
>
> for you in the multiplicity
>
> of your debacle. [. . .] (P 75)

He refuses to turn away from the fragmentation of his locale. To do so would only distance him further from the redeeming language that he seeks. Williams' frustration with his quest is apparent at the close of Section ii: "in your / composition and decomposition / I find my . . / despair!" (75). Despite his efforts to restore harmony through the creation of his poem, Williams perceives the continuing decay of his locale. His enjoyment of the "dusty fight" back in 1913, the conflict that started him on his poetic quest, has turned into "despair" as a result of his inability to reconcile the multiple divisions prevalent in this place.

Book II concludes with Paterson's descent from Garret Mountain. His descent signals Williams' use of a new line and measure:

> The descent beckons
>
>> as the ascent beckoned
>
>>> Memory is a kind
>
> of accomplishment
>
>> a sort of renewal
>
>>> even
>
> an initiation, since the spaces it opens are new
>
> places
>
>> inhabited by hordes
>
>>> heretofore unrealized, [. . .] (P 78)

These lines, which later appear as "The Descent" in *The Desert Music* (1954), illustrate Williams' conception of the variable foot. It represents the first time the variable foot "wholly satisfied" him (CP2 486). As he explains, it "brought about [. . .] my final conception of what my own poetry should be [. . .]" (IWWP 80).

Williams offers the following definition of variable foot: "The foot not being fixed is only to be described as variable. If the foot itself is variable it allows order in so-called free verse. Thus the verse becomes not free at all but just simply variable, as all things in life properly are" (82).

Along with the metrical innovation, Paterson's descent alludes to a familiar motif in Williams' work—a descent to make contact with the actual. In particular, it echoes the "Descent" chapter from *In the American Grain*. For Williams, Sam Houston takes a constructive approach to his locale because he "left everything behind him and took the descent once more, to the ground" (IAG 213). The young poet in "The Wanderer" also performs this symbolic act when he descends into the Passaic River. In his *Novelette*, Williams describes the importance of this symbolic descent. He claims that the poet must "progress downward to the beast. To the actual. To the devil with silks" (I 302). By descending to the "actual," Paterson thus attempts to overcome his distance from the lives of the people who struggle to survive in "Silk City."

With the closing of the Park and the departure of the "great beast," Faitoute leaves Garret Mountain unfulfilled. After all, "no poet has come" (P 79). The park reflects the breakdown evident during the day—flowers are "uprooted" and trees are "dismembered" (81). Faitoute tries to express the chaos he has observed:

> [. . .] he looks down, listens!
>
> But discovers, still, no syllable in the confused
>
> uproar: missing the sense (though he tries) (82)

Despite his persistence, he still has not discovered the language of the place. According to Doyle, "His pursuit of the `Beautiful Thing' at this stage is fruitless, as is his search for the 'redeeming language'. [. . .] [because of] his distaste for the actual 'local'" (115). He still gains comfort in "the thought of the stream" and the possibility of a marriage between word and place (P 82). However, his inability to express the Passaic Falls—to marry word and place—frustrates him. He is told to be "reconciled" with his world, but he insists, "the language is worn out" (84). He hopes that through his descent he will achieve his goal: "From that base, unabashed, to regain / the sun kissed summits of love!" (86).

Book II concludes with a lengthy letter from Marcia Nardi, whom Williams refers to as Cress throughout the poem. Cress's letter criticizes Dr. Paterson. She tells him that he is a writer "sheltered from life in the raw" and claims that he approaches literature and life with "two different inconsistent sets of values" (P 87). She argues that he fails to bring "life to literature" but only offers "purely literary sympathies and understandings" (90). She boldly exclaims:

> You've never had to live, Dr. P—not in any of the by-ways and dark underground passages where life so often has to be tested. The very circumstances of your birth and social background provided you with an escape from life in the raw; and you confuse that protection from life with an *inability* to live—and are thus able to regard literature as nothing more than a desperate last extremity resulting from that illusionary inability to live. [. . .]

Cress identifies the source of Paterson's frustration—his distance from the lives of the working people of the city. She goes on to criticize Dr. Paterson for his failure to offer "practical help." He lacks an understanding of her life in these "by-ways" of life: "all that takes a hell of a lot of money (especially for a woman)—a lot more than ten dollars or twenty five dollars" (89). She informs Paterson that economic problems not only affect laborers, but also the poet's creation of verse.

Williams' inclusion of this letter reflects his desire to present actual voices in his text. In a letter to Robert D. Pepper, he claims that Nardi's attack was "legitimate" and contained "a certain literary quality which was authentic [. . .]" (Weaver 209). He then goes on to explain his reason for using it:

> In the first place it was a reply from the female side to many of my male pretensions. It was a strong reply, a reply which sought to destroy me. If it could destroy me I should be destroyed. It was

just that it should have its opportunity to destroy. If I hid the reply
it would be a confession of weakness on my part.

Williams' use of this letter is crucial to the conclusion of Book II. As Margaret
Lloyd explains, the letter from Cress "brings together all of the themes which have
been interlaced throughout the first two books—divorce, economics, and the
moral obligation that a writer has to 'embrace the foulness' and 'life in the raw'"
(220). The letter also offers direction to Book III—it conveys the importance of
Paterson's "descent" into the "by-ways and dark underground passages" of his
locale (P 90).

Revisiting 1913 and the Power of the Masses

In Book III, "The Library," Paterson continues his search in the local
library. Echoing the frustration of the young poet in "The Wanderer," Paterson is
"[s]pent from wandering the useless / streets these months, faces folded against /
him like clover at nightfall [. . .]" (P 96). He looks for a refuge. He enters the
Library, as Sankey suggests, "to escape from the unremitting challenge of the
Falls, and to search in records of the past for the language he needs" (103). The
Falls, however, maintains its powerful hold over him—"still the roar in his mind
is / unabated" (P 97).

Williams organizes the three sections of Book III around the ideas of a
cyclone, fire, and flood:

> [. . .]   So be it. Cyclone, fire
> and flood. So be it. Hell, New Jersey, it said
> on the letter. Delivered without comment.
> So be it! (97)

The city of Paterson encountered all three of these natural disasters in 1902. In
regard to these disasters, Williams commented to Thirlwall: "I was moved, as
always, by the violence of history, which may be an accident, but still it gives
features to the otherwise pointless force of events" (309). Williams witnessed the

devastation of the fire and flood; he also observed the city's reconstruction. According to Mariani, this rebuilding taught Williams "a lesson in resiliency [. . .] a lesson Williams would never forget" (34).

In the context of this study's focus, one of the most significant references in *Paterson* occurs in the first section of Book III. After turning through old newspaper files, Paterson comes across a story about the razing of Lambert Castle:

> The "Castle" too to be razed. So be it. For no
>
> reason other than that it is *there*, in-
>
> comprehensible; of no USE! So be it. So be it.   (P 99)

Paterson's disbelief refers to several heated editorials that appeared in *The Prospector* during the mid-1930s that concerned the destruction of the castle's art gallery wing (Alaya 24). (By this time the Castle had been transferred to the Passaic County Park Commission and Historical Society.) At one time, Lambert's art gallery wing held one of the greatest private art collections in America, including works by Botticelli, Breughel, Rembrandt, Monet, and Renoir (22). On an 1898 visit to Lambert's Castle with President McKinley, Vice President Garret Hobart, who came from Paterson, remarked, "we have here the nucleus of an American Louvre" (18). Following the 1913 strike, however, Lambert sold his collection and by the winter of 1936 his gallery wing was destroyed. Paterson's response to this news reflects Williams' frustration with the willingness to destroy the past when it outlasts its utilitarian purpose.

After mentioning the partial destruction of Lambert's castle, Williams proceeds to describe the man:

> Lambert, the poor English boy,
>
> the immigrant, who built it
>
> was the first
>
> to oppose the unions: (P 99)

Lambert personifies the American "rags to riches" dream that has enticed so many to leave their homelands for America. As the son of English mill workers, he arrived in America at seventeen, worked for the silk manufacturer Anson Dexter, and within seven years he headed the firm (Alaya 3). Ironically, though he came from the working class, he fiercely opposed any action that this class took to assert its power. Williams expresses Lambert's tough attitude in the subsequent blocked verse:

> This is MY shop. I reserve the right (and he did)
>
> to walk down the row (between his looms) and
>
> fire any son-of-a-bitch I choose without excuse
>
> or reason more than that I don't like his face. (P 99)

Through this declaration of total power, Williams dramatizes the sense of ownership—both of capital and labor—that a man like Lambert possessed. Alaya claims that Williams' image is "exaggerated" (21). She describes Lambert as a "stern evangelist of the right of capital [. . .]" Regardless of his historical accuracy, Williams no doubt expressed the workers' view of this "stern evangelist" who refused to listen to them in 1913.

Lambert's refusal to negotiate with labor emerged clearly during the 1913 silk strike. As the owner of Dexter, Lambert, and Company, he flatly refused to deal with the strikers and their union. In *Silk and Sandstone*, Alaya recounts an incident between Lambert and Henry Doherty, whose workers had begun the strike. Hearing that his fellow manufacturer Doherty was ready to settle with the workers, an elderly Lambert reportedly "had to be restrained from striking him on the spot" (21). Such a response dramatizes Lambert's hostility towards labor. As Steve Golin notes, "Stubborn and willful, self-made men like Lambert preferred to risk their life savings rather than to compromise with a union" (77).

Williams juxtaposes Lambert's declaration of power and control with a direct reference to the 1913 silk strike and John Reed. This reference appears in an excerpt from a letter written by Robert Carlton Brown, a friend of Williams' since their Grantwood days. Williams kept in touch with Brown and even speculated with him in the New Llano Oil project, an investment failure (Mariani 349). Interestingly, he turned to Brown's letter about the 1913 strike when he experienced difficulty in moving *Paterson* along. In a letter to Brown, he explains that "*Paterson* III is stalled for the moment. I'm going to use your letter about Gurlie Flynn and the others in it" (P 281). Brown's letter thus acts as a catalyst for Williams—it puts him back in touch with the "dusty fight" that he first depicted in "The Wanderer," a poem he once described as the "genesis" of *Paterson*.

Brown's letter recounts several distinguishing features of the 1913 silk strike. He recalls the fact that he and his second wife Rose did not know one another when they went to Paterson. Like so many of the "intellectuals" who participated in the strike, they both "worked in the Pageant" (P 99). In regard to their other activities, Brown explains how "She [Rose] went regularly to feed Jack Reed in jail and I listened to Big Bill Haywood, Gurley Flynn and the rest of the big hearts and helping hands in Union Hall." Brown's letter recounts the memorable features of the strike: the innovative workers' Pageant, the activism of John Reed, and the participation of the prominent I.W.W. leaders. It shows the capacity for artists and laborers to overcome their differences and work together in an attempt to improve society—this union no doubt appealed to a poet searching for the redeeming language of the place. Brown's letter stands in direct opposition to the formidable depiction of Lambert's tyrannical power and control. When Williams next declares, "They broke him all right" (99), he makes it clear that this collective force had an impact on the absolute power wielded by Lambert. Alaya questions the accuracy of Williams' remark. She claims that World War I had a lot to do with Lambert's financial troubles; however, she does concede "the strike had hurt him [. . .]" (21). Steve Golin goes further: "Lambert could not recover from the strike [. . .]" (77). Despite Alaya's claims that "Lambert was not a man for breaking" (21), it appears that the workers' protest did break Lambert's control over them. Their strike thus portrays the potential power of the working class to overthrow a dominant form of power.

Yet Brown's final comment about "the damned thing now" suggests the ultimate inadequacy of the strike for lasting positive change (P 99). Outsiders, like Brown and Reed, did not stay to see the workers through with their ongoing fight. The victory over Lambert is thus symbolically incomplete, as evident in the fact that his castle, though partially razed, continues to stand. The strikers may have broken the man, but the economic structure, like his castle, remains in place.

Williams focuses on the castle in his next two stanzas. He describes Lambert as a "Limey" who arrived in America with "his head full of castles" (P 99). Determined to impose his English imagination on American soil, Lambert constructed a royal residence. What Lambert eventually built, according to Williams, was a "Balmoral on the alluvial silt, the rock-fall skirt- / ing the volcanic upthrust of the 'Mountain'." Thus, he constructed his dream on the region's "alluvial silt"—the soil deposited by the Passaic River. Williams pays specific attention to the castle's windows, particularly those "illuminated by translucent / laminae of planed pebbles" (100). Because the windows are made from local materials, they are the "most authentic detail / of the place" and remain its "best artifact."

Lambert's castle, as Alaya notes, "expressed an oddly assorted taste for all the stylistic idioms of Europe" (12). In this way, the castle represents Lambert's failure to make contact with the locale. Like Hamilton, Lambert came to this place and imposed his will on it—his shop, his workers, his castle. Kurt Heinzelman notes the significance of such economic imposition: "For Williams, the *imposition* of the imagination (Lambert's Balmoral-like castle, Hamilton's federal city) is the cardinal sin, for such grand *idees fixes* suppress the essence of imagination, its need for 'the continual and violent refreshing of the idea'" (252). Consequently, the strikers' ability to break Lambert's power offers a momentary outburst of the imagination.

Faitoute's ears ring while reading from "a roar of books" that oppresses him (P 100). His mind drifts to thoughts of the "Beautiful Thing." Her image contrasts with the "stagnation and death" that emanate from the books in the Library (101). Williams then describes the rape of the "Beautiful Thing" in a car, using lines from "Paterson: Episode 17." In contrast to the masses' power to break free from Lambert's control, this rape scene represents their capacity to perpetrate shocking violence against the "Beautiful Thing." Yet the "great beast" is not alone in this destructive brutality. A frustrated Faitoute, who is "haunted" by the "Beautiful Thing," also attempts to gain control over her while her "beauty is attainable" (105). He commands her to take off her clothes:

> (Then, my anger rising) TAKE OFF YOUR
> CLOTHES! I didn't ask you
> to take off your skin . I said your
> clothes, your clothes. You smell
> like a whore. I ask you to bathe in my
> opinions, the astonishing virtue of your
> lost body (I said) . (105-106)

He exhibits the same degree of crudeness as the guys from Newark in his attempt to possess her. As James Breslin contends, these lines reveal "how Paterson, in his demands for a pure beauty, is himself implicated in the maiming and violating of natural beauty" (193). His desire to shape and control this beauty threatens the essence of his quest.

He soon realizes that he cannot force the "Beautiful Thing" to "bathe" in his "opinions." His attempt to "know" her appears hopeless. A voice then asks,

> Doctor, do you believe in
> "the people," the Democracy? Do
> you still believe—in this
> swill-hole of corrupt cities?
> Do you, Doctor? Now?
>
> Give up

the poem. Give up the shilly-

shally of art. (P 109)

This questioning reveals the frustration of a poet "(ridded) from Paradise" who is struggling to continue his quest in this hell known as Paterson. After witnessing the exploitation, degradation, and rape of beauty in all corners of this place, he questions his search for "[t]he radiant gist that / resists the final crystallization." He refuses to give up the poem and continues to search for the redeeming language in the records of the past.

In the second section, which relates to the fire, Faitoute's search for the "Beautiful Thing" intensifies. He again envisions meeting her. This time he goes down to the basement "by the laundry tubs" where she recovers from her rape and beating (P 125). He recalls the image of "Persephone / gone to hell [. . .]" (126), which evokes his earlier experimental work *Kora in Hell.* Instead of attempting to possess her, he stares in "amazement" and admits that he is "shaken" by her beauty. Her brutal story then unfolds. He sees how her legs had been "scarred" since childhood "by the whip." "Instead of trying to force his righteous opinions upon her 'lost body'," Breslin contends, "he lets her physical being speak silently to him [. . .]" (194). In this way, he sees how she was brutalized by the guys from Paterson who "socked" her in the nose "for good luck and emphasis / cracking it" (P 127).

As the section concludes, Williams expresses his renewed effort to care for her, not control her, in his poem. He declares, "I can't be half gentle enough, / half tender enough / toward you [. . .]" (128). "In his leaning to care for Beautiful thing," Sergio Rizzo comments, "one imagines there is an alliterative association with the idea of Paterson learning to care as well" (56). Following his declaration to the "Beautiful Thing," as the dark flame continues to grow, Paterson ironically exclaims:

BRIGHTen

the cor

ner

where   you   are! (P 128)

Williams' syllabic emphasis, through capitalization and line breaks, illustrates his tenderness to the language he uses in trying to express this place. Peter Schmidt suggests that these closing lines reflect Dr. Paterson's "new willingness to find beauty in this world, not an ideal one of his own making" (185). His use of this popular revival hymn also foreshadows Billy Sunday's appearance in Book IV.

The final section of Book III describes the flood and its foul aftermath. The "muck" that remains once the river subsides is "a pustular scum, a decay, a choking / lifelessness [. . .]" (P 140). Paterson struggles "to begin again" on his quest as the "roar" of the Passaic Falls continues to draw him on. He admits,

> [. . .] I am its slave,
>
> its sleeper, bewildered—dazzled
>
> by distance . I cannot stay here
>
> to spend my life looking into the past: (145)

He has gained a more sensitive understanding of the "Beautiful Thing," but he has failed to discover a redeeming language in the books of the past. Such a closed reading of this place will not enable him to "comb out the language" of the present. The section ends with Paterson screaming "Let / me out! (Well, go!) this rhetoric / is real!" (145). As Doyle contends, "It is among people, and not books, that he must find the redeeming language" (127).

A Never-Ending Search

The industrialization and economic issues of *Paterson* emerge quite powerfully in Book IV Section i, which presents "An Idyl." In accordance with the river's movement to the sea, the Idyl takes place outside Paterson—in Manhattan. It includes three main personas: Corydon, a wealthy New York lesbian who fashions herself a poet; Phyllis, a masseuse who comes from the Ramapos and was trained in Paterson; and Dr. Paterson, a married man who consistently tries to consummate a sexual relationship with Phyllis. William Sharpe remarks, "The tangled sexual situation, with Phyllis as the teasing focus of both Dr. Paterson's adultery and Corydon's lesbianism, only underlies the distance from true Arcady" (148).

Corydon desires Phyllis. In an attempt to become more familiar, she talks to Phyllis about the city of Paterson.

> Paterson!
> Yes, of course. Where Nicholas Murray Butler was
> born   . and his sister, the lame one. They
> used to have silk mills there   .
> until the unions ruined them. Too bad. [. . .] (P 151)

Her associations with Paterson reveal her bias towards the working class. First, she associates Paterson with the birthplace of Butler, the renowned educator and president of Columbia University (1901-1945). Although Butler was not born in Paterson (he was born in Elizabeth, New Jersey), he did spend much of his early life in the city (Butler 44). He lived on the corner of Hamilton Avenue and Auburn Street, graduated from Paterson High School, and eventually even received an appointment to Paterson's Board of Education. No doubt Butler's numerous Hamiltonian associations evoked Hamilton's ghost for Williams. Besides living on Hamilton Avenue and presiding over Columbia University, Butler also delivered a speech in Paterson when a statue of Hamilton was unveiled in front of City Hall (59-60). Interestingly, a statue of Hamilton also stands in front of Hamilton Hall, the main undergraduate humanities building at Columbia. It is therefore not surprising that Corydon's next association to Paterson concerns the silk mills. She blames the unions for the failure of Paterson's silk industry. Such a declaration overlooks the numerous factors contributing to the decline in Paterson's silk industry, including the role manufacturers played in moving away for cheaper labor. Obviously, Corydon knows little about the locale (or even cares about it)—her only interest concerns making love to Phyllis.

Corydon fashions herself a poet. She recites several poems to Phyllis, one of which is addressed to a "dreamy / Communist" (P 159). She finally works up her nerve to recite "*Corydon, a Pastoral*" (160). When she finishes, Phyllis succinctly states, "It stinks!" (161). Her poetry has failed to reach her audience. Mariani classifies the situation in the following way: "it is Phyllis / Paterson / Williams—the raw, indigenous phase of the language, promising but as yet unfulfilled (a virgin)—confronting a heavily encrusted, symbol-laden, tradition-bound, and perverted phase of the language in the figure of Corydon" (617). Williams himself described Corydon as the "great world" and Phyllis as the "primitive world of the provincial city" (SL 304). He continually struggled over his allegiance to both places. As he wrote this section, he found that he gained affection for Corydon, as he lost interest in Phyllis. He candidly admits to Robert Lowell:

> I like the old gal of whom I spoke, she was at least cultured and not without feeling of a distinguished sort. I don't mind telling you that I started writing of her in a satiric mood—but she won me quite over. I ended by feeling admiration for her and real regret at her defeat. (SL 302)

Such a remark again indicates Williams' ambivalence towards the working-class—his initial desire to write of the common worker, but his ultimate preference for "cultured" figures.

When visiting Manhattan in "The Wanderer," the young poet sees "empty men" who jostle one another to stay above the gutter. His muse's appearance as an old prostitute further dramatizes the buying and selling going on here. In the context of this Manhattan setting in *Paterson*, Williams describes the incorporation of money making. He notes that it is in the tall buildings "where / the money's made" (P 164). He compares the workers to "plugs" and describes a "sanitary lunch hour" where workers sit: "expressionless, facing one another, a mould/ for all faces [. . .]" (165). These workers, like the strikers in "The

Wanderer," lose their humanity and individuality to their work environment. The place is different and the work is different, but the deadening effect on the workers remains the same.

Section ii develops the earlier Billy Sunday allusion. Williams juxtaposes an image of Madame Curie walking across the stage at the Sorbonne with Sunday yelling out "Come on up! Come up Sister and be / saved (splitting the atom of / bitterness)!" (P 171). As previously mentioned, Sunday's presence in Paterson factored into Williams' selection of the city for his epic. He declares, "I had heard Billy Sunday: I had talked with John Reed" (A 391). The spatial proximity of the Sunday and Reed references suggests their closeness in Williams' mind. As Mike Weaver first pointed out, Reed wrote a feature on Sunday for the *Metropolitan* in 1915 (215). Reed's article revealed that Paterson's silk manufacturers and clergy paid Sunday to preach to the silk workers. Sunday's secretary Mr. Ackley told Reed:

> You see, Paterson has always had the name of being a turbulent and unchristian city; and they think that Mr. Sunday will turn the thoughts of the working population to the salvation of their own souls, and regenerate Paterson. (12)

Williams explored such an alignment between clergy and manufacturers in his Ehrens-Hamilton juxtaposition in Book II. The payoff to Sunday, which Reed uncovered, provides Williams with a more sinister personification of such an alignment than Ehrens' preaching in the park.

Sunday's visit to Paterson generated a lot of commotion in the city. Prior to his arrival, Elizabeth Gurley Flynn reminded Paterson workers about the manufacturers' financial backing of Sunday's visit and warned them about his message. She exclaimed, "He will tell you that you are going straight to hell and try to make you forget that you are living in hell on earth right now" ("Says Sunday" 20). The I.W.W. decided not to actively protest Sunday's visit. According to one I.W.W. "scout," "The working element in Paterson has got Billy

Sunday's number. [. . .] They're taking care of Sunday in their own good way by giving him a cold frost" ("I.W.W. Not to Fight" 6). *The New York Times* did indeed report that initially Paterson was "cool to Billy Sunday" ("Paterson is Cool" 1), but by the time that he left the city in May he reportedly had made a record number of converts and received $25,000 ("Sunday Gets $25,000" 18). Nevertheless, the rumors surrounding Sunday's visit brought to light industry's use of religion to control the working-class.

Several features in Williams' portrayal of the preacher also appear in Reed's *Metropolitan* article: Sunday's proclamation "Come to Jesus!" (70); his movements like a baseball player (70); and the singing of "Brighten the Corner Where You Are" (68). Williams describes Sunday on stage as the "ex-rightfielder" and portrays him

> . as paid for
>
> by the United Factory Owners' Ass'n .
>
> . to "break" the strike
>
> and put those S.O.Bs in their places, be
>
> Geezus, by calling them to God! (P 172)

Interestingly, Williams conflates Sunday's visit with the 1913 strike. In his remarks on this episode, Mariani even discusses Sunday's visit "in 1913 to break the back of the long, drawn-out strike [. . .]" (620). Yet, Sunday did not visit Paterson in 1913 and at the time of his visit in 1915 workers were not out on strike (though threatening another walk-out). Thus, Williams makes the two events one—dramatizing the subversive tactics used by the manufacturers to breakdown the power of the working class.

Williams also portrays the manufacturer's corruption of Sunday and his message to the working people. As Joseph Riddel argues, "Billy *Sun*day is nominally an ev*angel*ist, the deliverer of the word, [. . .] but it is a word delivered into a prescribed situation, an energy perverted by usury to a perverse use" (240). Sunday thus portrays another corruption of the word associated with this place.

176

Williams describes Sunday:

> —getting his 27 Grand in the hotel room
> after the last supper (at the *Hamilton*)
> on the eve of quitting town, exhausted
> in his efforts to split (a split
> personality)   .   the plate   (P 172)

Significantly, Sunday receives his money in the Hamilton hotel. Such a powerful association did not go unnoticed by Williams. It further illustrates Hamilton's corrupting influence—even in 1915. In relating Sunday to Ehrens Mariani suggests, "we see this other evangelist, merging with the sons of Hamilton, in the act of 'quitting town,' having raped Paterson once again" (620). Sunday even has the audacity to close with the hymn "Brighten / . . the corner where you / are!" (P 172). Williams juxtaposes the hymn with the first of three letters from Allen Ginsberg. It is a letter, according to Ginsberg, "to make my presence in Paterson known to you" (172). Following this instance of exploitation and corruption, it no doubt brightened Dr. Paterson's corner to have another poet "in the same rusty county of the world." As Brian Bremen suggests, Ginsberg "represents the continuation of Paterson, both place and poem, in history" (196).

Before the section concludes, Williams turns to the subject of credit. In his review of *Paterson*, Randall Jarrell describes Williams' introduction of Usury and Credit as "those enemies of man, God, and contemporary long poems" (239). He claims that Williams has borrowed Pound's ideas: "he takes Credit and Usury over from Pound and gives them a good home [. . .]." Yet as Mike Weaver convincingly argues, "Pound had no monopoly of monetary reform ideas" (112). He references the fact that Williams' father supported Henry George's Single-Tax. In contrast to Pound, who "offered a blue-print for society," Weaver contends that Williams viewed economics as it relates to the "local materials of writing" (Weaver 113). Jay Rogoff has also worked to show that *Paterson* is not dependent on Pound's economic thought: "the poem dissonantly counters Pound at the same time as it appears to harmonize with him" (40). Williams attempts to search in the very nature of credit for the redeeming language. As John Ulrich contends,

> *Paterson* offers us much more than a mere reiteration of Social Creditism (or Poundism), for it is here that Williams articulates a visionary relationship between credit and money [. . .] Williams will align his vision of credit with the project of writing itself, with what he regards as the liberating aesthetics of discovery and invention. (122)

It is in his alignment of credit with his writing of *Paterson* that Williams looks to discover the language that can overcome the economic divisions that trouble his locale.

Williams first presents an advertisement by August Walters, which first appeared in *Money* June 1950 (Weaver 215). This advertisement, originally entitled "DO YOU FAVOR LENIN OR UNCLE SAM?," presents Walters' argument about reforming the U.S. finance system in order to beat the Russians and "win the cold war" (P 180). This finance plan relies upon the institutions of National Credit for banks and Banker's Credit for depositors. To gain a Social Credit perspective of Walter's plan, Mike Weaver contacted Gorman B. Munson, a former General Secretary of the American Social Credit Movement. Munson offers a critique of the plan:

> This is fiat money—no basis given for the creation of these producer credits. [. . .] Unsound. I cannot imagine Wms. approving of it. Contrast with social credit. S.C. is a distribution of purchasing power to everybody—not restricted to a few producers of war goods. [. . .] Finally the aim of Social Credit is to bring about economic democracy, not to beat Russia in the arms race. (215)

This financial reform advertisement thus presents a radical sounding voice who redefines money and credit in terms of the same old power structure. No wonder Williams follows the advertisement with the correlation, "MONEY : JOKE" (P 181). He makes this correlation again later in the section:

> Money : Joke
>
> could be wiped out
>
> at stroke
>
> of pen
>
> and was when
>
> gold and pound were
>
> devalued (P 184)

He exposes the arbitrary nature of money as a value system. As John Ulrich explains, "money is thus a joke in the sense that it is really nothing, nothing more than written language, and therefore readily modified, rewritten" (124). Jay Rogoff also focuses upon the power of the pen; he claims that it "can offer credit, relieving the public from the cruel practical joke of monetarism, but the stroke can also assert Williams' control over his own epic, devaluing Pound whenever necessary to maintain the poem's unique vision or technique" (40).

The monetary value system that rules contemporary society has distorted human values. This distortion appears clearly when Williams portrays the predicament of a poor man's hospitalization:

> Take up the individual misfortune
>
> by buffering it into the locality—not
>
> penalize him with surgeon's fees
>
> and accessories at an advance over the
>
> market price for
>
> "hospital income" (181)

The health care fees not only distort the true focus of the medical profession, but they show the need for some form of social credit. As this situation illustrates, credit must be available throughout the community and not controlled by specific people or institutions. The result of such monopolization has severe consequences for the community: "Money sequestered enriches avarice, / makes poverty: the direct cause of / disaster." This capacity for the rich to get richer while the poor become poorer widens the gap of social inequality and results in the socio-economic disaster prevalent throughout the city of Paterson.

Williams then correlates "Money: Uranium." He describes "usury" as a "cancer" destroying society and argues that the socialization of credit can combat the disease. He exclaims, "Release the Gamma rays that cure the cancer" (P 182). To clarify his view of money and credit, he offers the following metaphorical definition:

> What is credit?   the Parthenon
>
> What is money?   the gold entrusted to Phideas for the
>   statue of Pallas Athena, that he "put aside"
>   for private purposes
>
> —the gold, in short, that Phideas stole
>
> You can't steal credit : the Parthenon. (183)

By defining credit and money through these metaphors, Williams clarifies their difference. One is open to the community; the other has the potential to be hoarded by an individual. As John Ulrich explains, "credit is represented as the social, an ideal made manifest in a gathering place for the community in honor of Wisdom. Money, on the other hand, is represented as anything *but* the social; money is gold, matter, a commodity, appropriated and privatized by individuals" (122). Williams not only believes credit has the potential to destroy economic inequality, but that it has the potential to liberate the artist. As Williams espoused in his Social Credit speech, credit offers the artist a chance to produce art more freely. He voices this belief in *Paterson*: "credit, stalled / in money, conceals the generative / that thwarts art or buys it (without / understanding) [. . .]" (P 182).

By the close of the section, Williams moves beyond the "Money: Joke" correlation and associates credit with the discovery of radium: "credit: the gist"

(184). This credit/ radium association emphasizes the potential power linked to the process of discovery. Williams then connects this discovery process to Pound's call for "LOCAL control of local purchasing / power" (185). This "remedy" reinvests the locale with the power to address its own needs. As Sankey remarks, the concept of credit "will release the power latent in the New World, and in each locality" (193). The discovery of credit as "THE GIST" makes it possible for the community to overcome the division between "squalor" and "splendour" (P 185). It thus equates with the very nature of writing *Paterson* (127). In accordance with credit's regenerative power, Williams concludes the section by declaring that credit is "'the radiant gist' against all that / scants our lives" (P 185).

Although Williams intended *Paterson* to be a four book project, by Section iii of Book IV, as the river comes closer to emptying into the sea, he declares—"the sea is not our home" (199). The quest, the search for the redeeming language is not over. It can never be over. As Lloyd suggests, "The hero cannot achieve his quest because the need which a 'redeeming' language fulfills is constantly changing. The world is in a continual state of flux and no solution can be final" (277). The poet offers the only possible hope of expressing this flux. Williams remarks in a note to Book III, "The poet alone in this world holds the key to their final rescue" (P 279). Consequently, Book IV ends with Paterson emerging from the sea "headed inland, followed by the dog" (202). "Odysseus swims in as man must always do," Williams remarks, "he doesn't drown, he is too able but, accompanied by his dog, strikes inland again (toward Camden) to begin again" (P xiv).

"Reawakening the World": An Aged Poet's Return to Paterson

Book V of *Paterson*, published in 1958, portrays Williams "reawakening the world / of Paterson" (205). In commenting upon this book, he writes that

there can be no end to such a story I have envisioned with the

> terms which I had laid down for myself. I had to take the world of
> Paterson into a new dimension if I wanted to give it imaginative
> validity. Yet I wanted to keep it whole, as it is to me. (xv)

One of the primary images in the Book is the Unicorn. Williams identifies the
imaginative power of the artist with this mythical beast:

> The Unicorn
>
> has no match
>
> or mate . the artist
>
> has no peer (P 209)

Williams bases his image of the Unicorn upon the 15th-16th century Hunt of the
Unicorn tapestries displayed in the Cloisters Museum of New York. The image of
this tapestry functions as a central metaphor for the imaginative weaving together
of this book (perhaps, the whole poem). As Williams remarks in "Caviar and
Bread Again," the poet must gather together "all the threads [. . .] that have been
spun for many centuries" and weave them "into his design" (SE 103).

Book V portrays the aged Paterson's return to "the old scenes / to witness"
the changes that have occurred to this place (P 207). Despite the passing of time,
he sees that art has "SURVIVED!," especially in regard to the tapestries exhibited
in "*The Cloisters*." He comes upon the tapestry that depicts the wounding of the
Unicorn:

> lying wounded wounded on his belly
>
> legs folded under him
>
> the bearded head held
>
> regally aloft . (209)

However, this is not the end for the Unicorn or the aged poet. He contends that
the imagination, as manifested in art, "cannot be fathomed" (210). Its resistance
to total understanding marks its liberating nature. It thus transcends all forms of
restrictive structures—"It is through this hole / we escape." This "hole" ensures
the survival of the imagination, even beyond the death of the artist. At this point,

a letter from Allen Ginsberg appears in the text. Ginsberg's letter informs "Dr. Williams" about the publication of his poems and his departure for the North Pole—"I'll see icebergs and write great white polar rhapsodies" (210). Yet Ginsberg swears to Williams that he will return "to splash in the Passaic again" and "make big political speeches" (211). Like Williams, this other poet baptized in the Passaic refuses to turn away from the social troubles of the city—"Paterson is only a big sad poppa who needs compassion." The imagination continues to survive in a place where it is desperately needed. Ginsberg's letter provides a sense of continuance for the older poet: "now a younger man comes to a point where the journey can begin again" (Callan 183). Following Ginsberg's letter, Williams once again asserts the enduring nature of the imagination and exults in the willingness of artists, like Ginsberg, to "WALK in the world."

In Section ii of Book V, Ezra Pound, the artist as economist, lectures his friend "BilBill" on the source of America's fiscal problems:

> Wars are made to make debt, and the late one started by the ambulating dunghill FDR has been amply successful. [. . .] [Y]ou suckers had paid ten billion for gold that cd / have been bought for SIX billion. Is this clear or do you still want DEEtails? (216)

John Berryman refers to Pound's letter as "a page of economic junk" (qtd. Rogoff 40). Williams' juxtaposes Pound's sermonizing economic letter, which lacks "DEEtails," with a particular vision of a woman on the streets of Paterson. She appears in "worn slacks" and seems fairly plain: "her / face would attract no / adolescent" (217). Yet Paterson is attracted to her. He finds her physical presence unique: "she was dressed in male attire, / as much as to say to hell/ with you." He perceives her momentary capacity to bring together for him opposites like male and female. He pursues her until she "disappear[s] in the crowd" (217). He admits he has "a thousand questions" for her. He especially wants to know her "NAME" and to ask her, "have you read anything that I have written?" (218). He confesses, "It is all for you [. . .]." His pursuit of this woman on the streets of

Paterson reflects his life-long attempt to express the plain beauty he sees on the streets in his verse. It offers a reminder to the reader and Williams, as Jay Rogoff contends, "that in conjunction with the living language, 'Rigor of beauty is the quest,' not to be subordinated to economic concerns" (42). Williams' pursuit of this woman is therefore emblematic of his pursuit of the redeeming language: "The dream / is in pursuit" (P 219).

In the final section of Book V, Williams describes Peter Brueghel's *The Adoration of Kings* (1564). In this painting, Brueghel portrays the Holy Family amid a gathering of kings, soldiers, and other curious onlookers. Art critics H. Arthur and Mina C. Klein comment upon Brueghel's depiction of the scene:

> Every person, including Mary and Joseph, is plausible. They are human beings—ordinary, not extraordinary, homely and solid rather than glamorous or supernatural. [. . .] They are earthy, even coarse, individuals, but genuine rather than idealized; they have not ceased to breathe and sweat. (28)

Such an interpretation of Brueghel's figures could be applied to countless figures in Williams' verse. Not surprisingly, Williams focuses upon the ordinary quality of the people in Brueghel's painting. He simply refers to the Christ Child and the Virgin Mary as the "baby" and the "pretty girl" (P 224); he describes Joseph as "the pot bellied / greybeard (center)" (223). "It is a realistic portrait both artists give us," says Mariani, "rather than a mere sermon in paint" (708). Williams appreciates the genuine quality of Brueghel's work:

> —it is a scene, authentic
>
> enough, to be witnessed frequently
>
> among the poor (I salute
>
> the man Brueghel who painted
>
> what he saw— (P 223-224)

Brueghel's image of mother and child rings true with the twentieth century poet/ doctor who entered countless homes of the poor. Its "authentic" quality conveys the timeless power of such art to touch others. In Brueghel's painting, Williams evokes an artistic tradition that represents his own worldly aesthetic.

Brueghel's "ordinary" depiction of the Holy Family also displaces the traditional power structure of the scene. The Kleins note this feature of the painting:

> King or carpenter, magistrate or stablehand, soldier or saint—all are offered with equal simplicity, directness, and candor. Nothing is ornamented or elaborated. Nothing is distorted into an appearance of luxury or aristocratic sophistication. (28)

The ability to bring together these diverse figures again reflects one of Williams' principal aims in the multi-voiced text of Paterson. The ordinary depiction of these figures, however, also results in Brueghel's capacity to bring together opposites. Since the Holy Family appears in this ordinary light, the "pretty girl" can be read as both Virgin Mary and adulterous whore; the child can be seen as the Son of God and bastard; the "old man in the / middle" can be seen as saint and cuckold—he is after all "the butt of their comments" (P 223). The three kings, whom Williams simply refers to as "3 men," can be seen as "highwaymen" who have "stolen" the gifts, "works of art," they present to the child (224; 225). These kings "saw with their proper eyes" the value of this child. Yet a violent tension exists between the kings and "the vulgar soldiery" who look on in "envy" (225). As Terence Diggory notes, violence towards authority "persists in the presence of the Soldiers" (45). Brueghel manages to present the opposition and tension in this one scene:

> Peter Brueghel the artist saw it
> from the two sides: the
> imagination must be served—
> and he served
>
> > dispassionately (225)

Williams saw it too. He found in this painting's "authentic" tone the potential of the imagination to bring together the multiple, contrasting representations of humanity. As Margaret Lloyd explains, the entire Book is "primarily concerned with the fusion of opposites and of seemingly irreconcilable differences in attitude (old age/ youth; past/ present; virgin/ whore; life/ death; male/ female) through the power of the imagination" (267). Williams' description of Brueghel's painting thus encapsulates his ongoing struggle to serve the imagination "dispassionately."

Williams' own effort to regenerate the "big sad poppa" forces him to confront the social troubles of the city, specifically the desire for wealth that Hamilton instilled here. Immediately following his declaration about Brueghel, Williams declares, "It is no mortal sin to be poor—anything but this featureless / tribe that has the money now— [. . .]" (225). Money continues to corrupt this place and its people. It has produced a low-grade society. Echoing his criticism of contemporary America in *The Great American Novel*, Williams declares, "we have come in our time to the age of shoddy, the men are / shoddy, driven by their bosses, inside and outside the job to be / done, at a profit" (P 225). Despite his perception of this "shoddy" culture, the aged poet will not turn away—"the / imagination must be served." He will continue "living and writing" (227); after all, he remains "possessed by many poems" (228).

By the close of Section iii, the aged poet returns to the source of his imaginative birth—the river:

> "the river has returned to its beginnings"
>
> and backward
>
> (and forward)
>
> it tortures itself within me
>
> until time has been washed finally under:
>
> and "I knew all (or enough)
>
> it became me   . " (229)

These lines are paraphrases or direct excerpts from the "Saint James' Grove" section of "The Wanderer" when the young poet's muse baptizes him into the

Passaic River. The change to the present tense in the verb "tortures" reflects the fact that his immersion in this river has stayed with him for over forty years. As he declared in 1914, "it became me." For Williams, the river and the man are one. Although "the times are not heroic / since" he emerged from the polluted river, he claims that "they are cleaner / and freer of disease" (230).

As the section closes, Williams invokes his grandmother muse from "The Wanderer." The connection between the poems is heralded by the crows' cry: "Caw! Caw! Caw!" (234). He recalls,

> She was old when she saw her grandson:
>
> You young people
>
> think you know everything.
>
> She spoke in her Cockney accent
>
> and paused
>
> The past is for those that lived in the past. Cessa! (P 235)

His grandmother spoke the final line, according to Williams, "with a dirty look in her eye" (292). At the close of this latest Book, Williams thus once again revisits the point of his poetic awakening. Like she did throughout "The Wanderer," the muse instructs him—she tells him to avoid an immersion in the past. Such an immersion will be certain death for him. She tells her poet that the "measure is all we know." This line articulates the knowledge he has gained on his quest. He concludes,

> We know nothing and can know nothing
>
> but
>
> the dance, to dance to a measure
>
> contrapuntally,
>
> Satyrically, the tragic foot. (P 236)

Like the flow of the river, this dance, with its satyr-like quality, embodies the continuous movement in language that Williams struggles to express. Williams remarked about these lines: "That has to be interpreted; but how are you going to interpret it?" (Koehler 17). He envisioned a musical dance: "I always think of the Indians there. [. . .] The Indians had a beat in their own music, which they beat with their feet." Although he has yet to capture the redeeming language of this place, Williams understands that its continual flux constitutes its beauty.

Paterson VI was posthumously published; it is only a fragment and represents the aged and sick poet's continuation of his quest. Although the book contains just a few pages, it touches upon some subjects pertinent to this study. First, it opens by addressing Alexander Hamilton:

> you knew the Falls and read Greek fluently
>
> It did not stop the bullet that killed you—close after dawn
>
> at Weehawken that September dawn (P 237)

This address suggests that Williams still has not overcome Hamilton's presence as it relates to his poem. By invoking Aaron Burr's shooting of Hamilton, Williams seems to be re-imagining the violence required to destroy the man whom he blames for corrupting the "roar" of the Passaic Falls. Book VI also relates the stories of two lower-class women. He writes of Lucy who was sold to Charlie "for 3 hundred dollars" and gave birth to 13 children (P 240). He describes her as "vulgar / but fiercely loyal to me." He also refers to Mrs. Blackfinger "who could tell a story / when she'd a bit taken." These references suggest that Williams was not done looking for the glimpses of "beauty" in the lives of the working-class people who have made-up his locale.

Even though Book VI is an unfinished fragment, it illustrates Williams' conception of *Paterson* as a never-ending quest. Williams refused to turn away from the challenge of the Falls' "roar." Such a choice would have conflicted with his sense of duty as a poet to discover the redeeming language of the place. It also would have opposed his notion of *Paterson* as an open, evolving modernist poem that resists closure. In the end, Williams' continuing work on *Paterson* represents his return to the "filthy" Passaic River and its perpetual promise of "new wandering" (CP1 36).

CONCLUSION

The 1913 Paterson silk strike was a significant event in the annals of American labor history. This struggle between local silk manufacturers and laborers exposed some of the deep social and economic divisions prevalent in American society during the early part of the twentieth century. In response to the technological and labor demands of the manufacturers, silk workers—crossing ethnic and religious lines—stood together in opposition to a working environment where they had no voice and consequently no power. For six months, as John Reed declared in "War in Paterson," the city was a battlefield between capital and labor. Seeing the larger possibilities of how this local conflict could transform the nation, the radical Industrial Workers of the World and many intellectuals from Greenwich Village joined the strikers' struggle. They were opposed by an influential group of silk manufacturers who exerted considerable control over the local Paterson authorities. The 1913 strike thus brought into conflict diverse strands of American society.

Besides drawing together this unique collection of people, the 1913 strike also resulted in a unique form of expression by John Reed and the Paterson strikers—The Paterson Pageant. With his use of local Paterson strikers as actors, Reed enabled the strikers to tell their story. For one night in New York City, the workers expressed to the world their working conditions and the consequences of their attempt to speak out. As with any war, both sides suffered casualties. Yet, the city—Hamilton's industrial dream—survived and continued to suffer.

Not only did the strike attract the attention of diverse groups of people, but it also captured the imagination of Williams Carlos Williams who was living in nearby Rutherford, New Jersey. Prior to the strike, Williams wrote traditional verse that comes across, for the most part, as disconnected from his immediate experience of industrialized Northern New Jersey. A distinct change to his poetry occurs, however, following the 1913 silk strike. Nowhere is this change more apparent than in the central section of his poem "The Wanderer," entitled "Paterson—The Strike." In this section, Williams portrays the young poet's journey through the streets of Paterson during the 1913 silk strike and his contact with a group of strikers patiently waiting on a bread-line. Although he is sympathetic to these men and women, the young poet is repulsed by the brutality of their lives. Williams' stereotypical representation of them reflects his own crude class sensibilities. Nevertheless, the violence of their "dusty fight" enables him to emerge as a poet connected to his locale.

After the publication of "The Wanderer," Williams intensified his efforts to represent his locale in his poetry. In *Al Que Quiere!*, he presents several lower class subjects. Too often, however, Williams' control over their representation results in a patronizing tone in the poems. With the creation of his experimental works *Kora in Hell* and *Spring And All*, Williams manages to break free from this tendency to dominate his subject and presents interplay between multiple voices. His artistic experiments in *The Great American Novel* and *In the American Grain* also reflect his exploration of the historical and contemporary materials available to the American artist. Many times he portrays the crudeness and vulgarity of these materials, but he continually makes use of them to offer a composite portrait of the contemporary American scene.

The "Paterson—The Strike" section from "The Wanderer" reverberated throughout Williams' growth and development as a poet. He continually returned to Paterson in both his poetry and prose and struggled to represent this locale. While working out this epic project, Williams also struggled with the political dimensions of his art. He pursued some radical interests, like the Social Credit Movement, but he refused to commit himself to party work. As his wife Flossie declares, "Bill isn't a radical or a communist or anything else. He's an honest man. And if he gets into it with both feet, it's just too bad" (Koehler 24). Williams constantly evaded limiting political definitions and continued to pursue the creation of his "magnum opus." He made several poetic attempts leading-up to *Paterson*, which resulted in several key features of his long poem: the idea of a city/ man, the "Beautiful Thing," and the rhythmic quality of colloquial language. These shorter "Paterson" poems portray a poet not only experimenting to find a form, but also a poet sensitive to the many voices inherent in his locale.

Paterson embodies Williams' epic effort to express the poetry of this local place. Reminiscent of Reed's pageant back in 1913, Williams uses local materials—both verse and prose—that allows the many disparate voices of this place to tell their story. He weaves together these materials in an attempt to harmonize the discordant voices and discover a redeeming language for this place. His search for this language involves a return to his earlier "Paterson" poetry, including "The Wanderer." It also involves a return to Paterson's volatile labor history, specifically the 1913 silk strike. By revisiting his earlier work and this particular event, Williams touches the mainspring of his origins as a modern American poet. The brutality of the "dusty fight" had seeped "deep into the blood" of Williams. It made him "listen clearer" not only to his muse, but to the working people of Paterson as he searched to discover the redeeming language of his locale. Like its lasting impact on the city of Paterson, the 1913 silk strike continued to affect William Carlos Williams long after the workers went back to their jobs in the silk mills.

WORKS CITED

Adams, Graham, Jr. *Age of Industrial Violence 1910-1915: The Activities and Findings of the United States Commission on Industrial Relations.* New York: Columbia UP, 1966.

Ahearn, Barry. "The Poet as Social Worker." *William Carlos Williams Review* 19.1-2 (1993): 15-32.

---. *William Carlos Williams and Alterity: The Early Poetry.* New York: Cambridge UP, 1994.

Alaya, Flavia. *Silk and Sandstone: The Story of Catholina Lambert and His Castle.* Paterson: Passaic County Historical Society, 1984.

Aleksa, Vainis. "Modernist Dialogue: William Carlos Williams in the Magazines, 1915-1925." Diss. University of Illinois at Chicago. 1994.

Anderson, Sherwood. *Selected Letters.* Ed. Charles E. Modlin. Knoxville: U of Tennessee P, 1984.

Barry, Nancy K. "Epic History and the Lyric Impulse in the *Paterson* Manuscripts." *William Carlos Williams Review* 12.2 (1986): 1-8.

---. "The Fading Beautiful Thing of Paterson." *Twentieth Century Literature* 35 (1989): 343-363.

Blair, Stanley Scott. *The Poetry, Life, and Times of the Young William Carlos Williams.* Diss. Duke University, 1993. Ann Arbor: UMI, 1994. 6194.

Bremen, Brian. *William Carlos Williams and the Diagnostics of Culture.* New York: Oxford UP, 1993.

Breslin, James E. *William Carlos Williams: An American Artist.* New York: Oxford UP, 1970.

Butler, Nicholas Murray. *Across the Busy Years.* New York: Charles Scribner's Sons, 1939.

Callan, Ron. *William Carlos Williams and Transcendentalism: Fitting the Crab in a Box.* New York: St. Martin's Press, 1992.

Clifford, James. *The Predicament of Culture: Twentieth-Century Ethnography, Literature, and Art.* Cambridge: Harvard UP, 1988.

Coles, Robert. "Instances of Modernist Anti-Intellectualism." *Modernism Reconsidered.* Ed. Robert Kiely. Cambridge, MA: Harvard UP, 1983. 215-228.

Conarroe, Joel. *William Carlos Williams' Paterson: Language and Landscape.* Philadelphia: U of Pennsylvania P, 1970.

Conrad, Bryce. "Engendering History: The Sexual Structure of William Carlos Williams' *In the American Grain.*" *Twentieth Century Literature* 35 (1989): 254-278.

Diggory, Terence. *William Carlos Williams and the Ethics of Painting.* Princeton: Princeton UP, 1991.

Doyle, Charles. *William Carlos Williams and the American Poem.* New York: St. Martin's Press, 1982.

Dunn, Allen. "Williams's Liberating Need." *Journal of Modern Literature* 16:1 (1989): 49-59.

Eastman, Max. "Jack Reed—A Memoir." *The Complete Poetry of John Reed.* Ed. Jack Alan Robbins. Washington, D.C.: UP of America, 1983. 70-80.

--. "*The Masses* and the Negro." Editorial. *Echoes of Revolt: The Masses 1911-1917.* Ed. William L. O'Neill. Chicago: Quadrangle Books, 1966. 232-233.

---. *Venture.* New York: Albert & Charles Boni, 1927.

Fiero, F. Douglass. "Williams Creates the First Book of *Paterson*." *Journal of Modern Literature* 3.4 (1974): 965-986.

"Find Editor Guilty in Paterson Trial." *New York Times* 4 June 1913: 1+.

Finkelstein, Norman M. "Beauty, Truth, and *The Wanderer*." *William Carlos Williams: Man and Poet*. Ed. Carroll F. Terrell. Orono, ME: National Poetry Foundation, 1983. 233-242.

Fisher-Wirth, Ann W. *William Carlos Williams and Autobiography: The Woods of His Own Nature*. University Park: Pennsylvania State UP, 1989.

Flynn, Elizabeth Gurley. "The Truth About the Paterson Strike." *Rebel Voices: An I.W.W. Anthology*. Ed. Joyce L. Kornbluh. Ann Arbor: U of Michigan P, 215-226.

Frail, David. *The Early Politics and Poetics of William Carlos Williams*. Ann Arbor: UMI Research Press, 1987.

Goldberg, David J. *A Tale of Three Cities: Labor Organization and Protest in Paterson, Passaic, and Lawrence, 1916-1921*. New Brunswick: Rutgers UP, 1989.

Golin, Steve. *The Fragile Bridge: Paterson Silk Strike, 1913*. Philadelphia: Temple UP, 1988.

Green, Martin. *New York 1913: The Armory Show and the Paterson Strike Pageant*. New York: Charles Scribner's Sons, 1988.

Hamilton, Alexander. "The Report on the Subject of Manufacturers." *The Papers of Alexander Hamilton*. Ed. Harold C. Syrett. Vol. 10. New York: Columbia UP, 1966. 230-340.

Heinzelman, Kurt. *The Economics of the Imagination*. Amherst: U of Massachusetts P, 1980.

Homberger, Eric. John Reed. New York: Manchester UP, 1990.

---. "Proletarian Literature and the John Reed Clubs, 1929-1935." *Journal of American Studies* 13 (1979): 221-244.

"I.W.W. Not to Fight Sunday." *New York Times* 11 Apr. 1915: 6.

Jarrell, Randall. "A View of Three Poets." rpt. in *William Carlos Williams: The Critical Heritage.* Ed. Charles Doyle. Boston: Routledge & Kegan Paul, 1980. 238-241.

Jay, Paul. "American Modernism and the Uses of History: The Case of William Carlos Williams." *New Orleans Review* 9.3 (1982): 16-25.

Johnston, John H. *The Poet and the City: A Study in Urban Perspectives.* Athens, GA: U of Georgia P, 1984.

Kemp, Harry. *More Miles: An Autobiographical Novel.* New York: Boni and Liveright, 1926.

Klein, H. Arthur and Mina C. Klein. *Peter Bruegel the Elder: Artist of Abundance.* New York: MacMillan Co., 1968.

Kornbluh, Joyce L. *Rebel Voices: An I.W.W. Anthology.* Ann Arbor: U of Michigan P, 1965.

Kreymborg, Alfred. *Troubadour.* 1925. New York: Sagamore Press, 1957.

Lawson, Andrew. "Divisions of Labour: William Carlos Williams's `The Wanderer' and the Politics of Modernism." *William Carlos Williams Review* 20.1 (1994): 1-22.

Lloyd, Margaret Glynne. *William Carlos Williams's Paterson: A Critical Reappraisal.* Rutherford: Fairleigh Dickinson UP, 1980.

Lowney, John. *The American Avant-Garde Tradition: William Carlos Williams, Postmodern Poetry, and the Politics of Cultural Memory.* Lewisburg: Bucknell UP, 1997.

McDonald, Forrest. *Alexander Hamilton: A Biography.* New York: W.W. Norton, 1979.

McLewin, Philip J. "Labor Conflict and Technological Change: The Family Shop in Paterson." *Silk City: Studies on the Paterson Silk Industry, 1860-1940.* Newark: New Jersey Historical Society, 1985. 135-158.

Macksey, Richard A. "`A Certainty of Music': Williams' Changes." *William Carlos Williams: A Collection of Critical Essays.* Ed. J. Hillis Miller. Englewood Cliffs, NJ: Prentice-Hall, 1966. 132-147.

Mariani, Paul. *William Carlos Williams: A New World Naked.* 1981. New York: W.W. Norton, 1990.

Marsh, Paul Alec. "The 'Money Question' and the Poetry of Ezra Pound and William Carlos Williams." Diss. Rutgers U, 1993.

Miller, J. Hillis. *Poets of Reality: Six Twentieth- Century Writers.* Cambridge, MA: Belknap Press of Harvard UP, 1965.

Miller, James E. *The American Quest for a Supreme Fiction:* Whitman*'s Legacy in the Personal Epic.* Chicago: U of Chicago P, 1979.

Miller, John C. *Alexander Hamilton: Portrait in Paradox.* New York: Harper & Brothers, 1959.

Murphy, Margueritte S. *A Tradition of Subversion: The Prose Poem in English from Wilde to Ashbery.* Amherst: U of Massachusetts P, 1992.

Naumann, Francis M. and Paul Avrich. "Adolf Wolff: 'Poet, Sculptor and Revolutionist, but Mostly Revolutionist." *The Art Bulletin* 67.3 (1985): 486-500.

Nochlin, Linda. "The Paterson Strike Pageant of 1913." *Art in America* May/June 1974: 64-69.

Palattella, John. "But If It Ends The Start is Begun: *Spring and All*, Americanism, and Postwar Apocalypse." *William Carlos Williams Review* 21.1 (1995): 1-21.

"Paterson is Cool to Billy Sunday." *New York Times* 5 Apr. 1915: 1.

"Paterson Strikers Now Become Actors." *New York Times* 8 June 1913: 2.

Pinsky, Robert. "American Poetry and American Life: Freneau, Whitman, Williams." *Shenandoah* 37.1 (1987): 3-26.

Poole, Ernest. *The Harbor.* 1915. New York: Macmillan, 1928.

Pound, Ezra. *Pound/ Williams: Selected Letters of Ezra Pound and William Carlos Williams.* Ed. Hugh Witemeyer. New York: New Directions, 1996.

Procopiow, Norma. "Tradition and Innovation in William Carlos Williams' *The Great American Novel.*" *Modernist Studies: Literature and Culture 1920-1940* 4 (1982): 160-175.

Ray, Man. *Self Portrait*. Boston: Little, Brown and Co., 1963.

Reed, John. "Back of Billy Sunday." *Metropolitan* May 1915: 9+.

---. "Program of the Paterson Strike Pageant." *Rebel Voices: An I.W.W. Anthology*. Ed. Joyce L. Kornbluh. Ann Arbor: U of Michigan P, 1965. 210-212.

---. "War in Paterson." *John Reed for The Masses*. Ed. James C. Wilson. Jefferson, NC: McFarland & Co., 1987. 26-34.

---. "Whose War?" *John Reed for The Masses*. Ed. James C. Wilson. Jefferson, NC: McFarland & Co., 1987. 164-166.

---. "A Word to Mr. Pound." Letter. *Poetry: A Magazine of Verse* 2.3 (1913): 112-113.

Rev. of "Pageant of the Paterson Strike." *Survey* June 1913. rpt in *Rebel Voices: An I.W.W. Anthology*. Ed. Joyce L. Kornbluh. Ann Arbor: U of Michigan P, 1965. 213-214.

Riddel, Joseph N. *The Inverted Bell: Modernism and the Counterpoetics of William Carlos Williams*. Baton Rouge: Louisiana State UP, 1974.

Rizzo, Sergio. "The Other Girls of Paterson—Old and New." *William Carlos Williams Review* 20.1 (1994): 38-60.

Rogoff, Jay. "Pound-foolishness in *Paterson*." *Journal of Modern Literature* 14.1 (1987): 35-44.

Rosenstone, Robert A. *Romantic Revolutionary: A Biography of John Reed*. New York: Random House, 1975.

"Sanctions Against Williams." *Partisan Review* 3.4 (1936): 30.

Sanger, Margaret. *Margaret Sanger, an Autobiography*. 1938. New York: Dover Publications, 1971.

Sankey, Benjamin. *A Companion to William Carlos Williams's Paterson*. Berkeley: U of California P, 1971.

"Says Sunday is Paid to Oppose Workers." *New York Times* 17 Mar. 1913: 20.

Schmidt, Peter. *William Carlos Williams, the Arts, and Literary Tradition.* Baton Rouge: Louisiana State UP, 1988.

Schonbach, Morris. *Radicals and Visionaries: A History of Dissent in New Jersey.* Princeton: D. Van Nostrand Company, 1964.

Scranton, Philip B. Introduction. *Silk City: Studies on the Paterson Silk Industry, 1860-1940.* Newark: New Jersey Historical Society, 1985.

Sharpe, William. *Unreal Cities: Urban Figuration in Wordsworth, Baudelaire, Whitman, Eliot, and Williams.* Baltimore: John Hopkins UP, 1990.

Sinclair, Upton. *American Outpost: A Book of Reminiscences.* 1932. Port Washington, NY: Kennikat Press, 1969.

"Socialism and Strikes." Editorial. *New York Times* 16 May 1913: 10.

Stecchini, Catherine. Personal interview. 12 June 1997.

Steffens, Lincoln. *The Autobiography of Lincoln Steffens.* New York: Harcourt, Brace, and Co., 1931.

Stokes, Rose Pastor. "Paterson." *Echoes of Revolt: The Masses 1911-1917.* Ed. William L. O'Neill. Chicago: Quadrangle Books, 1966. 89.

"Storm the Court For Labor Trial." *New York Times* 8 May 1913: 1.

"Strikers Make Demonstration at Funeral in Paterson, N.J." *Rutherford Republican* 17 May 1913: 3.

"Sunday Gets $25,000 and Charity $6,000." *New York Times* 24 May 1915: 18.

Tapscott, Stephen. *American Beauty: William Carlos Williams and the Modernist Whitman.* New York: Columbia UP, 1984.

Tashjian, Dickran. *William Carlos Williams and the American Scene 1920-1940.* Berkeley: U of California P, 1978.

"The Temptation of Dr. Williams." *Partisan Review* 4.2 (1938): 61-62.

Thirlwall, John C. "William Carlos Williams' "Paterson": The Search for the Redeeming Language—A Personal Epic in Five Parts." *New Directions in Prose and Poetry* 17 (1961): 252-310.

Townley, Rod. *The Early Poetry of William Carlos Williams*. Ithaca: Cornell UP, 1975.

Tripp, Anne Huber. *The I.W.W. and the Paterson Silk Strike of 1913*. Urbana: U of Illinois P, 1987.

"Two Pageants—A Contrast." Editorial. *New York Times* 9 June 1913: 8.

Ulrich, John. "Giving Williams Some Credit: Money and Language in *Paterson*, Book Four, Part II." *Money: Lure, Lore, and Literature*. Ed. John Louis DiGaetani. Westport, CT: Greenwood P, 1994.

Von Hallberg, Robert. "The Politics of Description: W.C. Williams in the 'Thirties," *ELH*, 45 (Spring 1978), 131-151.

Wagner, Linda Welshimer. *The Prose of William Carlos Williams*. Middletown, CT: Wesleyan UP, 1970.

Wallace, Emily Mitchell. *A Bibliography of William Carlos Williams*. Middletown, CT: Wesleyan UP, 1968.

Weaver, Mike. *William Carlos Williams: The American Background*. Cambridge: Cambridge UP, 1971.

Wertheim, Arthur Frank. *The New York Little Renaissance: Iconoclasm, Modernism, and Nationalism in American Culture, 1908-1917*. New York: New York UP, 1976.

Whitaker, Thomas R. *William Carlos Williams*. New York: Twayne, 1968.

Whittemore, Reed. *William Carlos Williams: Poet from Jersey*. Boston: Houghton, 1975.

"Who is the Leader?" *Rebel Voices: An I.W.W. Anthology*. Ed. Joyce L. Kornbluh. Ann Arbor: U of Michigan P, 1965. 204.

Williams, Ellen. *The First Ten Years of Poetry, 1912-1922*. Urbana: U of Illinois P, 1977.

Williams, William Carlos. "America, Whitman, and the Art of Poetry." *The Poetry Journal* Nov. 1917: 27-36.

---. "The American Idiom." *New Directions in Prose and Poetry* 17. 1961. 250-51.

---. *The Autobiography of William Carlos Williams.* 1951. New York: New Directions, 1967.

---. *The Collected Poems of William Carlos Williams, Vol. 1: 1909-1939.* Eds. A. Walton Litz and Christopher MacGowan. New York: New Directions, 1986.

---. *The Collected Poems of William Carlos Williams, Vol. 2: 1939-1962.* Ed. Christopher MacGowan. New York: New Directions, 1986.

---. *The Collected Stories of William Carlos Williams.* 1961. New York: New Directions, 1996.

---. *I Wanted to Write a Poem: The Autobiography of the Works of a Poet.* 1958. New York: New Directions, 1978.

---. *Imaginations.* Ed. Webster Schott. New York: New Directions, 1971.

---. *In the American Grain.* 1925. New York: New Directions, 1956.

---. Interview with Stanley Koehler. *Writers at Work: The Paris Review Interviews.* 3rd Series. New York: Viking Press, 1967.

---. *Interviews with William Carlos Williams: "Speaking Straight Ahead."* Ed. Linda Welshimer Wagner. New York: New Directions, 1976.

---. *Paterson.* Ed. Christopher MacGowan. New York: New Directions, 1992.

---. *A Recognizable Image: WCW on Art and Artists.* Ed. Bram Dijkstra. New York: New Directions, 1978.

---. *The Selected Essays.* 1954. New York: New Directions, 1969.

---. *The Selected Letters of William Carlos Williams.* Ed. John C. Thirlwall. New York: McDowell, Obolensky, 1957.

---. "A Twentieth-Century American." *Poetry: A Magazine of Verse* 47.4 (1936): 227- 229.

---. *William Carlos Williams and James Laughlin: Selected Letters.* Ed. Hugh Witemeyer. New York: W.W. Norton, 1989.

Wolff, Adolph. "Songs, Sighs and Curses." *The Glebe* 1.1 (1913): 1-84.

"Writer Sent to Jail." *New York Times* 29 Apr. 1913: 1

INDEX

MELLEN STUDIES IN LITERATURE:
POETIC DRAMA AND POETIC THEORY

Volumes 1 thru 221 were printed as Salzburg Studies in English Literature/Poetic Drama and Poetic Theory.

For further information please contact The Edwin Mellen Press.